COPTIC ORTHODOX
PATRIARCHATE

MANY YEARS

WITH PEOPLE'S QUESTIONS

PART IV

Dogma and Ritual Questions

By
H.H. POPE SHENOUDA III

Title	: Many Years With People's Questions Part IV.
Author	: H. H. Pope Shenouda III.
Translated By	: Mrs. Glynis Younan - London.
Revised By	: Mrs Wedad Abbas.
Illustrated By	: Sister Sawsan.
Edition	: The First edition - August 1992.
Typesetting	: J. C. Center, Heliopolis.
Printing	: Dar El Tebaa El Kawmia, Cairo.
Legal Deposit No.	: 5896 /1992
Revised	: COEPA - 1997

H.H. Pope Shenouda III
117th Pope and Patriarch of Alexandria
and the See of St Mark

INTRODUCTION

I am continuing, dear Reader, with publishing for you a collection of questions which I have received, either in the weekly meetings on Wednesdays (formerly Fridays), or which students at the Theological College (the Seminary) have addressed to me during my lectures.

This, the fourth part of the series **Many Years with the Problems of People**, which you now have in your hands, is concerned with theological, doctrinal and ritual questions.

It contains the replies to some 60 questions divided up as follows:

a) **37 questions on faith and theology, up to page 108**

b) **12 or so questions on ritual theology, up to page 132**

c) **10 questions about the Virgin Mary provoked by various statements of the Plymouth Brethren, from page 134 to the end.**

The first part of this whole series consists of questions concerning the Holy Bible (40 questions in all), while the second centres on theological and doctrinal questions (35 questions), the third part addresses spiritual and general questions (44 questions), and in this fourth part I answer the following 60 questions.

So far then, if we count the whole series altogether I am replying to some 179 questions.

I have tried to make the answers as short and to the point as possible and to support them with texts from the verses of the Bible.

I look forward to meeting you again in the fifth part, if God wills.

Pope Shenouda III

[1]

THE SPIRITS AND THEIR WORK

Question

Are there spirits who work in this world? And if so, what are they like?

Answer:

Spirits were created in two types; the spirits of angels and the spirits of human beings. The angels are also of two types: holy angels, and evil angels or demons. There is no doubt that both types, good and bad, are at work in the world. It was said of the angels: "*Are not all angels ministering spirits sent to serve those who will inherit salvation?* " *(Heb. 1:14)* and "*The angel of the Lord encamps around those who fear Him, and delivers them.* " *(Ps. 34:7)*

The work of the demon spirits is to corrupt mankind spiritually, but only if people surrender their wills to them, or to throw some or take possession of them. This is why the Lord gave His disciples and saints the gifts of casting out demons. *(Matt. 10:1, 8; Mark 16:17)*

As far as the spirits of mankind are concerned, the wicked end up imprisoned in hell, while some of the righteous become entrusted by God to provide help for their brothers on earth, and these spirits may even appear to those people as Virgin Mary and St. George do.

[2]

CAN THE SPIRITS RECOGNISE EACH OTHER?

Question

Can the spirits recognise each other while they are in the place of waiting?

Answer:

Yes, of course. There is no doubt that they can. And we have the clear example of this in the story of the rich man and the poor Lazarus, where the Bible says that after they had both died, the rich man:

"looked up and saw Abraham far away, with Lazarus by his side. So he called to him, 'Father Abraham, have pity on me'." (Luke 16:23).

We notice here that the rich man knew which was Lazarus and which was Abraham, and we also see that Abraham knew that one of them had received his blessings on earth, while the other had suffered troubles.

Therefore it is clear from this that a spirit's capacity to recognise extends to those whom the person has seen before as well as to those whom he has not.

For the rich man not only recognised Lazarus whom he had seen with his own eyes in the world, while he was alive, but he also recognised Abraham whom he had never met or ever set eyes on. In the same way our forefather Abraham recognised both of them.

The knowledge of the spirits become very extensive after they have become separated from the body.

Thus we find our master St Paul saying: *"Now we see but a poor reflection as in a mirror; then we shall see face to face. Now I know in part; then I shall know fully, even as I am fully known". (1Cor. 13:12).*

[3]

"NO-ONE HAS EVER SEEN GOD"

Question

What is the meaning of the verse, "*No-one has ever seen God***"? (John 1:18) Has not God appeared to many of the prophets and spoken to them?**

Answer:

What is meant by 'God' in this phrase is the god head, His essential divinity, because this god head is invisible. And in regard to this divinity since God is Spirit, He cannot be seen by our earthly eyes which can only perceive material things.

This is why God always appeared in the form of a human being or in the shape of an angel when it was intended for human beings to see Him. And finally He appeared in the body when we saw Him in His Son Jesus Christ who said: "*Anyone who has seen Me has seen the Father.* " *(John 14:9)*

Thus after John the Baptist said "*No-one has ever seen God*", he went on to say: "*The Only Begotten Son, who is in the*

Father's bosom, has made Him known. " (John 1:18), which means that He declared the Father.

All those who try to depict or have ever tried to portray the Father in a visible form, have got it wrong, and this very verse proves them wrong, for example those who portray the Father in icons of the baptism of Christ, when God said: *"This is My Son, whom I love; with Him I am well pleased."" (Matt. 3:17)*, when no-one actually saw the Father.

All the while that we are in this physical body, there is a mist like a veil preventing us from seeing God, we can only see *"a poor reflection as in a mirror. "* as St Paul put it *(1 Cor. 13:12)*. But when we put off this earthly body, we will be clothed in a shining, spiritual body that can see what no eye has ever seen. And it is then that we shall see God.

[4]

HOW CAN SPIRITS SEE SPIRITS?

Question

How can a spirit see another spirit? And does a spirit have a shape?

Answer:

There is a kind of spiritual perception by which the spirit can see beyond the limits of the body and its form, and by which it can also see God, as a spirit without form, in a vision that cannot be expressed as the Bible tells us: *"Blessed are the pure in heart, for they will see God. " (Matt. 5:8)* and as Job said: *"now my eyes have seen You." (Job. 42:5)*.

St Anthony saw the soul of Anba Amun being conducted to heaven by angels, and told this to his disciples. But what did he actually see?!

The rich man saw Abraham and Lazarus, but what exactly did he see, and in what form did he see them? Was it in the same way as St Anthony saw the soul of Anba Amun, and in the same form? I wonder whether the spirit can take on the shape of a body, without it being material or substantial!

We know that the angels of the Lord encamp around those that fear Him and deliver them, but we don't see the angels with the physical, bodily eye because they are spirits, and we can only see them by our own spirits. In his revelation, St John the Beloved, when he was *"in the Spirit"*, *"on the Lord's Day"* *(Rev. 1:10),* saw an angel directing him, and also saw other angels. But what did he actually see? Was it a spiritual vision beyond the level of form? Or did the angels also have a discernible shape?

There are angels who have taken on certain forms and been visible.

There were, for example, the angels of the Resurrection: on one occasion two angels appeared who were like, *"two men in clothes that gleamed like lightning. " (Luke 24:4),* and on another occasion the angel of the Lord appeared and, *"His appearance was like lightning, and his clothes were white as snow. " (Matt. 28:3)*

In the face of all this, St Augustine stood in wonder thinking over an important question, 'Does a spirit have a form? Or can it take on a form?', and he replied quite frankly, 'I do not know'.

Nevertheless we hear that the Cherubim and Seraphim have six wings, that with two of them they cover their faces, with another two their feet and with the remaining two they fly. Are all these just symbolical or metaphorical? Or do they actually have this shape, by which they can be distinguished, albeit in non-material form?

In regard to the eyes of the earthly body, the spirit obviously cannot be seen at all unless it takes on the kind of shape which the angels usually take on. But spirits see spirits, and often see them in definite form. I must add, though, that this is my personal view.

But we still have no answer to the question put by St Augustine.

As far as we know, at the Resurrection, bodies will rise and be united with spirits, and obviously these bodies will have shapes, and the same ones as they had before, but they will be 'spiritual' and 'imperishable' *(1 Cor. 15)* and will have no defects...

Are we to understand from this that the spirit has the same shape as the body? Or is it without a shape but then assumes the shape of the body?

There are things which the Bible does not explain, but which have been left for individual interpretation and conclusion.

I think it is most probable that spirits have shapes by which they can recognise one another and be distinguished from each other.

Even with these forms, though, they would still, in their spirituality, be far removed from physical, material forms.

[5]

THE CROWN OF RIGHTEOUSNESS

Question

Since Adam and Eve fell while they were in Paradise, is it possible that any of us would fall in the next world?

Answer:

No, of course not, for the nature in which we will rise after death, will be better in every respect than the nature which Adam and Eve had.

As far as the body is concerned, we will rise in a non-physical body, a spiritual, luminous, glorious body, a strong and indestructible one that resembles the glorious body in which Christ Himself rose *(Phil. 3:21),* according to St Paul, who also said: *"Just as we have borne the likeness of the earthly man, so shall we bear the likeness of the Man from heaven. " (1 Cor. 15:42-49).*

This body will not sin, because sin is a kind of corruption: *"It is sown in corruption, it is raised in incorruption. " (1 Cor. 15:42).* There will be no sin in the next world, for we are told about the heavenly Jerusalem that *"Nothing impure will ever enter it. " (Rev. 21:27).*

Here on earth we possess a will which can incline itself either to good or to evil. But in the kingdom of God, the will would only ever incline itself towards the good. This is because our wills will be sanctified when we put on the crown of righteousness.

St Paul said, concerning this crown: *"Now here is in store for me the crown of righteousness, which the Lord, the righteous Judge, will award to me on that day -and not only to me, but also to all who have longed for His appearing. " (2 Tim. 4:8)*

But what is this crown of righteousness?

It is the crown that gives us righteousness as a nature and makes us not sin any more.

As an example of this we have those holy angels whose wills successfully stood their tests, and who did not fall into corruption with Satan. For this they were crowned with righteousness and their wills were made sinless.

At present we can misuse the freedom granted to us by God. We can now desire with this freedom to do what is wrong, and to actually do it. But in eternity, the only desire we will have will be for God alone, and thus it will be impossible for us to sin. What is more, the very knowledge of evil will also fade from our minds entirely and we will enjoy perfect simplicity and total purity. We will be 'like God's angels in heaven'.

Now we have a knowledge of good and evil, but then we will know only the good.

We will only have knowledge of what is good, and we will love it and live it and our memories will be completely purified from all previous knowledge concerning what is evil. Thus we will be crowned with righteousness.

[6]

WHO ARE THE SERAPHIM?

Question

Who are the seraphim and what do they do?

Answer:

The word 'seraphim' is plural, the singular is 'seraph', and this word is used for a particular kind of angel, all of whom have six wings, with two of which they cover their faces, with another two their feet and with the remaining two they fly.

The particular passage in which the Bible refers to the seraphim is to be found in Isaiah, when the prophet saw these angels around the throne of God, praising Him and saying; *"Holy, holy, holy is the LORD of hosts; The whole earth is full of His glory!" (Is. 6:3).*

The work of the seraphim is to praise, even so, when they heard Isaiah cry, *"Woe to me!... I am ruined! For I am a man of unclean lips"*, one of the seraphim flew down *"with a live coal in his hand, which he had taken with tongs from the altar".* And he touched Isaiah on the mouth and said: *" Behold, this has touched your lips; Your iniquity is taken away, And your sin purged " (Is. 6:7).*

There is no mention anywhere in the Bible that any of the seraphim has ever fallen.

The literal meaning of the word ' seraphim' is 'the burning ones' or 'the ones who blaze with fire'. And it is clear from their name that they symbolise the divine love and love that never fails.

[7]

JUSTIFIED FREELY BY HIS GRACE

Question?

Since the Bible says we are *"justified freely by His grace "* *(Rom. 3:24),* then salvation must be free. So why do we associate it with baptism which is an act that has to be performed?

Answer:

The expression *"justified freely"* means that we do not have to pay a price for this justification. This is because *"the wages of sin is death. " (Rom. 6:23),* as it says in the same epistle to the Romans, and the Lord Christ paid this price for us with His death, by shedding His blood on the cross.

We, therefore, obtain justification without having to pay the price ourselves, hence it is free.

Baptism, however, is not the price, but the means to this justification.

For example, our Protestant brothers and sisters say that we are saved through faith. But faith is the means, and not the price. The price is nothing other than the blood of Christ; as the Bible says: *"without the shedding of blood there is no forgiveness. "* (Heb. 9:22) and the Lord Christ joined these two means; faith and baptism, together, when He said: *"He who believes and is baptized will be saved; "* (Mark 16:16)

It is not we who linked salvation with baptism, but the Lord Christ Himself and also the Holy apostles like St Peter who, when speaking about Noah's Ark, said *"in it only a few people, eight in all, were saved through water, and this water symbolises baptism that now saves you also. "* (1 Pet. 3:20-21)

And St Paul also said: *"He saved us, not by works of righteousness which we have done, but according to His mercy He saved us, through the washing of regeneration and renewing of the Holy Spirit ."*(Titus 3:5)

Perhaps you might object, saying: So if I am not baptised I will perish, and yet Christ died for my sake?

Christ certainly died for you, but you will need to follow the course which the Lord Himself laid down for your salvation. For this will be the means by which you gain that salvation which Christ has offered to you free.

In spite of the blood of Christ, is it possible to be saved, for example, without repentance?

Christ's blood alone is sufficient for salvation, but there are also His words: "*I tell you, no; but unless you repent you will all likewise perish.*" *(Luke 13:3 and 5)* Repentance isn't a price that has to be paid for salvation, but rather an essential means by which one can receive the justification which was won by the blood of Christ.

Baptism is also an essential and requisite part of being justified freely through Christ's blood. The Lord Jesus Christ Himself said: "*Most assuredly, I say to you, unless one is born of water and the Spirit, he cannot enter the kingdom of God.*" *(John 3:5)*

And faith, too, is another vital and necessary means whereby one can obtain that free justification which was won by Christ's blood.

Thus we have to differentiate between the price and the means.

The cost of justification was the blood of Christ alone. And the necessary and vital means whereby we can attain it are faith, baptism and repentance.

St Peter linked these three means together on the Day of Pentecost after the Jews believed and were cut to the heart. When they asked him what they should do, St Peter answered them: "*Repent, and let every one of you be baptised in the name of Jesus Christ for the remission of sins; and you shall receive the gift of the Holy Spirit.*" *(Acts 2:38)* So here we have the three means: faith in the name of Jesus Christ, repentance and baptism.

All these are means, but the one and only price paid for justification was the blood of Christ, and He alone paid that on our behalf.

We obtain this justification for free since we haven't paid anything for it. By which I mean that we haven't had to give our blood for it.

We gain it through faith, baptism and repentance, the three means to justification combined. They are simply the means while the only price paid for justification was Christ's blood.

It is then that we can enter into good works, which are the fruit of faith and repentance, and the result of the activity in us of the Holy Spirit which we have received through the sacrament of the holy chrism and the renewal and sonship which we were given at baptism.

Speaking of this righteousness, St John said:

" If you know that He is righteous, you know that everyone who practices righteousness is born of Him." (1 John 2:29).

The Lord Jesus Christ paid a price for your justification, and that was His blood. And He gave you this for free so that you wouldn't have to pay for it ever again. All you need to do is to follow the course to obtain it which our Lord Himself defined.

In order to explain this to you a bit further, I could say for instance: Let us suppose that you have a cheque for a very large amount of money, which you have perhaps acquired **freely,** as a result of an inheritance, but which you haven' yet been to the bank to collect as money. Obviously you still don't possess this sum, even though it is credited to you, because you haven't yet been through the procedures for realising it.

I will say it just once more: the price paid for justification was the blood of Christ-that and nothing else! And we obtain that justification freely, by way of faith, baptism and repentance.

[8]

CONCERNING THE JEWISH RELIGION

Question

Some people say that Judaism is a worldly, materialistic religion. What is your view on this assertion, and if it is true, has Christianity rectified the materialism of Judaism?

Answer:

Since Judaism is a heavenly religion, we can't describe it as being materialistic. And since the doctrines of Judaism were inspired by God in the Bible, that is in the Torah, we cannot describe God's commandments as being materialistic, otherwise we would be making an accusation against God Himself, and not only against God but against the great prophet Moses, who was the first to give mankind a divine written law. Could we ever accuse Moses of leading the people towards materialism?

The exalted nature of the teachings of Judaism could provide scope for many books, and we might be able to produce something of this later on. We also ought not to forget that much of what is said in the Books of the Old Testament Cannot be correctly understood without a knowledge of its symbols.

Someof those who criticise Jewish teachings, have not yet understood them properly.

To describe the Judaism as it is practised by the Jews as being materialistic is one thing, but to describe the Jewish religion in those same terms is something else entirely which could have serious consequences. For the Jews, after all, are human beings, they can make mistakes and go astray like anyone else. But the Jewish religion is from God: anything that does it an injustice is doing an injustice towards God who created it and also towards the mighty Moses through whom it came to man from God. It would also be to wrong the Torah which is an integral part of Judaism, and which God revealed as guidance and a light for His people. It wouldn't make sense if God were to send a prophet with a religion that would lead the people to materialism, would it?

The commandment to pay tithes in Judaism is totally opposed to materialism.

Judaism instructs that a tenth of all one's possessions should be paid to the Lord, a tenth of everything, *"whether grain from the soil or fruit from the trees, "* and a tenth *"of the herd and flock. " (Lev. 2 7:30,32) " You shall truly tithe all the increase of your grain that the field produces year by year." (Deut. 14:22)* And they also had to give their wheat. *(Deut. 12:17)*

In addition to the tithes, Judaism also enjoined the payment of the first fruits.

And what was meant by that, was the first of any form of produce, whether it was human offspring or a crop from the earth, or produce from the trees or from the flocks of sheep or cattle.

The Lord said: " *Consecrate to Me all the firstborn, whatever opens the womb among the children of Israel, both of man and beast; it is Mine.* " *(Ex. 13:2)*

So the first of anything born from livestock, from the flocks and herds belonged to the Lord, and the firstborn males from among the people were to be presented to serve the Lord, until the Levite tribe replaced these firstborn males.

The Jewish law also said *"The first of the first fruits of your land you shall bring into the house of the LORD your God. You shall not boil a young goat in its mother's milk."* *(Ex. 23:19)*, and " *bring a sheaf of the first fruits of your harvest to the priest."* *(Lev.23:10).* It also told the people to bring to the priests the first fruits of their grain, new wine and oil, and the first wool from the shearing of their sheep *(Deut. 18:4)*. The people were also asked to present a cake from the first of their ground meal, as an offering from the threshing floor. *(Num. 15:20)*. This day of the first fruits was held as a holy festival.

As far as fruit trees were concerned, for the first three years their fruit was to be considered forbidden, and the fourth year's fruit was all to be given to the Lord *(Lev. 19:24)*. Its owner could only eat of its produce the following year.

Would this remarkable offering be characteristic of a materialistic religion?

There were also the vows and free will offerings which people gave. *(Deut. 12:17)*.

One of the humanitarian aspects of the Jewish holy law is to be found in the Lord's instruction: " *When you reap the harvest of your land, you shall not wholly reap the corners of your field when you reap, nor shall you gather any gleaning from your harvest. You shall leave them for the poor and for the stranger: I am the LORD your God.* " *(Lev. 23:22)*. So the poor would be able to gather something to sustain them from behind the harvester.

Another of the humanitarian points of the Jewish law which shows that it was anti-materialistic was the freeing of slaves.

In the time of Moses and before, there was slavery, but the Jewish law commanded that they release in the seventh year any slave whom they had bought with their own money, who had served them for six years. *(Deut. 15:12)*

Another anti-materialistic feature of Judaism was the presentation of sacrifices and burnt offerings.

These were all aimed to please the Lord and to obtain forgiveness, and to atone for one's sin. These are all described in detail in the Book of Leviticus.

In some of the sacrifices, like the burnt offerings and the various sin offerings, the person presenting them was not allowed to take anything from them at all. One could not call this a materialistic concept for in fact it was a very spiritual one, involving being sorry for one's sins and offering repentance for them and sacrificing something material in order to atone for them - and all these things that were offered had their spiritual symbols.

Yet another anti-materialistic aspect of Judaism were the many religious celebrations, both weekly and yearly, which were holy days, that is,. days regarded as holy to the Lord, upon which the people did not work.

The Ten Commandments included the command to keep the Sabbath holy: " *the seventh day is the Sabbath of the LORD your God. In it you shall do no work: you, nor your son, nor your daughter, nor your male servant, nor your female servant, nor your ox, nor your donkey, nor any of your cattle, nor your stranger who is within your gates, that your male servant and your female servant may rest as well as you. And remember that you were a slave in the land of Egypt,...* " *(Deut. 5:14)*

Besides this there were more than twenty days of sacred holidays and festivals on which no activity was allowed unless it was spiritual, as we are told in Leviticus *(chapter 23)*.

If Judaism were materialistic, it wouldn't have designated some 73 days a year as holy days, that is exactly a fifth of a year - on which no work was to be done.

As far as their rules of prayer, hymns and holy readings were concerned:

There were seven daily prayers *(Ps. 119:164),* apart from the night prayers and the approaching of the House of God, which was done with singing and psalms, referred to as the Songs or Psalms of Ascents. The Torah was divided into a regular system of readings in the synagogues, so that all the people could hear it.
The spirituality contained in the teachings of Judaism, however, is a long subject which we do not have time to go into here.

[9]

PRAYING FOR THE DECEASED

Question

Can a Christian who dies in a state of sin enter the kingdom of heaven? I don't see how he can. So what is the use of praying for someone who has died when we don't know whether he has died in a state of sin or repentance?

Answer:

We don't have to pray for someone who has died whilst sinning. Prayer will not benefit him, and our master St John said: *"There is sin leading to death. I do not say that he should pray about that."* *(1 John 5:16)*.

If a thief climbs up the walls of a house in order to burgle it, and falls down and dies in the process, the Church would not pray for him. And if drug smugglers get into a fight with the police and get killed during this fight, the Church does not pray for them either. And if a person who has an intelligent mind and commits suicide, the Church does not pray for him.

Therefore, if the Church can be sure that the person has died whilst in the act of committing a sin, it doesn't pray for him.

But in other cases, it would certainly pray for someone who had died, so that he could at least depart from the world having been absolved by the Church, so that he is no longer bound in any way. That person is then left to the mercy of the One who searches men's hearts and the One who knows all secrets.

It is as if the Church is saying to God: this person has been released from our side by the authority to loose and bind which You gave to us *(Matt. 18:18; John 20:23)*, and so we leave him now to Your mercy and to Your knowledge which is beyond ours.

The Church also prays on behalf of the one who is passing on, for him to be forgiven any sins which he may have committed which weren't of the degree that leads to death, according to the instruction of the apostle.

As an example of this St. John said: " *If anyone sees his brother sinning a sin which does not lead to death, he will ask, and He will give him life for those who commit sin not leading to death. There is sin leading to death. I do not say that he should pray about that. All unrighteousness is sin, and there is sin not leading to death. " (1 John 5:16-17)*

So what are these sins that do not lead to death?

They are uncompleted sins, sins that have not been fully carried out. They may be sins of ignorance, sins committed unintentionally, or sins that are latent, or sins of negligence, for example.

We pray in the Trisagion saying:

[Forgive, absolve and pardon us, O God, for the wrongs we have done intentionally, those we have done knowingly, and those we have done unknowingly, the secret and the open.]

But unintentional sins, sins of ignorance and unseen sins are nevertheless still sins (because they violate God's commandments and require forgiveness and prayer).

In the Old Testament, we see that even in the case of sins committed unintentionally without knowing, as soon as one became aware, one had to offer a sacrifice so that they might be forgiven. *(Lev. 4:2,13,22-23)*.

The Church prays that the Lord would forgive any of these sins of ignorance or of negligence, or any sins committed unintentionally and unknowingly, which those who have passed over might have committed.

The Reciter says in the psalm: *"Who can understand his errors? Cleanse me from secret faults. " (Ps. 19:12)* It is for these hidden faults which the person is not aware of having, that the Church asks forgiveness on his behalf.

Let us suppose that a person has died suddenly without having had a chance to confess, or that he has forgotten to confess some sins, and therefore hasn't received an absolution for them. The Church can give him absolution and asks forgiveness for him, in the Prayer for the Departed.

The Church, therefore, prays for the sake of the departed out of a kind of compassion, because no-one is without sin, even if his life on earth lasts only one day (and this is a phrase which comes in part of the Prayer for the Departed).

David said: "If You, O Lord, kept a record of sins, O Lord who could stand? But with You there is forgiveness... " (Ps. 129:3-4) And he also said: *" Do not enter into judgment with Your servant, For in Your sight no one living is righteous. " (Ps. 143:2)* So if this is the situation, that there is no servant without a fault, and no master who is not forgiving, we pray for those who have passed away [Being human beings who put on the body and lived in the world].

We pray for everyone in this state, since only God is good. We ask for forgiveness and then leave the matter to God, always knowing that any human being might perhaps have repented even if it was at the hour of his death.

But for those who have died in the act of committing a deliberate sin, without having repented, we do not pray, since our prayers in these circumstances would be going against God's goodness and justice.

[10]

IS THERE AN ETERNITY FOR THE WICKED AND FOR SATAN?

Question

I have heard that eternity is an attribute of God alone, and that there isn't any eternal life for the wicked. For if there were an eternal life for evil, for the wicked and for the Devil, it would mean that Satan would then become a god, and people could then claim that two gods existed: a God of Good and a god of Evil! What is the opinion of the Church on this matter?

Answer:

It is the attribute of infinity, not just eternity (or having an existence after death), which belongs to God alone.

God is infinite, which means that He had no beginning. No other being has this quality, for all other beings have been created. Consequently they had a beginning at some point, and had no existence before that beginning. They are, therefore, necessarily finite, because at some point they did not exist. And since they were created they cannot be infinite.

Eternity in the form of eternal life, however, is something which God has given to some of His creatures.

God created human beings with an immortal soul, both the righteous and the wicked are alike in this respect.

This potential for immortality doesn't mean that human beings are gods, they are still human beings, in spite of the fact that God has bestowed on them eternal life. If eternal life were one of God's attributes alone, it would be impossible for a human being to live on after death and enjoy eternal life, because a human being cannot turn himself into a god.

Existence in an afterlife is for both the righteous and the wicked, but they will differ in their fate, as the Bible tells us concerning the Day of Judgement: *"Then they* (ie. the wicked) *will go away to eternal punishment, but the righteous to eternal life. " (Matt. 26:46)*

If we did not believe in this eternal existence for the wicked, we would on one hand be contradicting the Bible, and on the other we would be becoming like the Seventh Day Adventists who believe that the punishment of the wicked is non existence and annihilation.

This painful eternity is also for Satan and his angels.

The Bible says that on the Day of Judgement the Lord, *"will say to those on His left, " 'Depart from Me, you cursed, into the everlasting fire prepared for the devil and his angels " (Matt. 25:41)*

And the Book of Revelation says about Satan's punishment..
"The devil, who deceived them, was cast into the lake of fire and brimstone where the beast and the false prophet are. And they will be tormented day and night forever and ever. " (Rev. 20:10)

The phrases 'for-ever and ever' and 'eternal fire' mean that Satan and the wicked will live for-ever, but in torment.

Those who belong to the Jehovah's Witnesses and the Seventh Day Adventists, however, deny this.

[11]

DID GOD NEED CHRIST IN ORDER TO CREATE AND TO SAVE MANKIND?

Question

I heard a critic suggesting that, when He was creating the world, God needed Christ, so that the creation could take place, and that it says: *"Through Him (ie. Jesus Christ, being the Word) All things were made through Him, and without Him nothing was made that was made." (John 1:3).* Did God need Jesus Christ when it came to saving the world? And if this is so, does it not mean that God is not omnipotent?

Answer:

If God had needed anyone else to do these things, He could hardly be considered Almighty!!

But He is far beyond needing anyone else.

In the creation, everything was created at God's word, through the Word or Logos, who is God's mental power speaking for Him, or the speech of God expressing His Wisdom. All this was so, long before the incarnation, and before the creation of Adam and Eve and the entire world.

Since God was able to create everything through His own intellect or wisdom, or by His, word, He could not have needed to create anyone else in order to help Him.

The phrase 'God created the world' or 'the intellect of God created the world' or 'God created the world through His intellect', all point to one and the same meaning. God and His mind are one being, and the same goes for salvation.

It is God who has saved the world, without needing anyone else's help to do so.

If someone other than God had saved the world, salvation would not be boundless enough to redeem all people in every age from all their sins.

The real problem, though, for the person who makes this criticism is the incarnation.

The incarnation is a long subject, which we don't have time for here. In any case, it is not a matter for criticism.

That critic whom you mentioned, is trying to make out that God needed someone else to help in His plans, and that needing someone else would suggest that God was not Almighty. The answer to this, however, is that God never needed anyone else, either when it came to the creation, or the salvation of mankind. It is God who created everything, and He who redeemed all.

[12]

THE RELATIONSHIP OF THE APOSTLES WITH THE HOLY SPIRIT

Question

Were all the Apostles supported by the Holy Spirit? And on this basis did the Lord Christ have the same relationship with the Holy Spirit as the apostles had?

Answer:

The apostles had a relationship with the Holy Spirit because the Holy Spirit - according to the Creed - was the One who 'spoke through the prophets'.

But the relationship that the Lord Christ had with the Holy Spirit was hypostatic and quite distinct from that of the apostles or anyone else with the Spirit. This is because Christ's relationship with the Holy Spirit is eternal, and is based on equality.

Christ's relationship with the Holy Spirit existed before the creation of the world, before all ages, before time and from infinity, while none of the apostles had this same kind of relationship.

Christ abides in the Holy Spirit, and the Holy Spirit abides in Him, and both are ever-present in their mutual essence. They are of the same nature. This is the point on which Christ differed from all others in His relationship with the Holy Spirit.

Then again it was Christ who sent the Holy Spirit to the holy disciples, so that it came upon them on the day of Pentecost, and gave them the gift of speaking in tongues. None of the apostles could ever have said that he had sent the Holy Spirit.

[13]

HOW CAN I TELL WHICH LEAFLETS ARE ORTHODOX AND WHICH ARE NOT?

Question

I recently received some leaflets containing various spiritual words and religious teaching, which were mostly to do with redemption and salvation. How can I tell if these leaflets are genuinely Orthodox, especially in view of the fact that some of them say that they have been published by this or that 'Orthodox ' association or society?

Answer:

Just having the word 'Orthodox' attached to that society or association is not enough.

Many people conceal their own teachings behind the word 'orthodox'. Some people claim that they and their work are Orthodox, but because these people have been reading too many books that are not on Orthodox Christianity. And because these people attend non-Orthodox meetings and societies, and have formed close friendships with the non-Orthodox ideas which do not at all accord with the belief and faith of the Church. These ideas have entered their minds and shaped their opinions. Yet even so, they go ahead and publish these ideas.

So how can you tell the difference? Actually you can tell by the language, for what is genuinely Orthodox writing shows itself clearly in the language. According to what I have seen, of some of these pamphlets, I could say to you that in general:

Leaflets that are not truly Orthodox very often avoid mentioning the Church, the Sacraments and the priesthood, in whatever teaching they are trying to explain.

So for instance when writing about the forgiveness of sins, or repentance, or salvation or eternity, these kinds of publications just concentrate on the relationship between the individual and God, without bringing into it the activity of Church, the sacraments and the priesthood.

Frequently what they are saying unfolds in the following sequence of argument, for example they stress the importance of eternity, your need for salvation, that God loves you and that He alone can save you, therefore you must take refuge in God, open your heart to Him and receive Him as your Saviour etc. All this they expound without any mention of confession, receiving the Holy Communion, or the role of the Church.

Another observation which can be made is that these pamphlets for the most part talk to the readers as if those readers were doomed to destruction, as if they had not yet received redemption, and they talk to them about the blood

of Christ, as if those readers had not so far gained its effectiveness in their lives.

And the final irony is that these unorthodox groups distribute their leaflets at the doors of churches while those within these churches have already experienced atonement for their sins through Christ's blood, on the day that they were baptised.

[14]

CONCERNING THE DIVINITY OF CHRIST

Question

Are there any verses in the Bible that clearly state Christ's divinity? I would appreciate it if you could mention some of them.

Answer:

Yes, of course. There are many verses, among which we could cite:

✣ The words of St Paul concerning the Jews: *"Theirs are the patriarchs, and from them is traced the human ancestry of Christ, who is God over all, for ever praised! Amen ". (Rom. 9:5)*

✣ The beginning of John's gospel states it plainly too, when it says: *" In the beginning was the Word, and the Word was with God, and the Word was God. " (John 1:1)* And in the same chapter, John attributes the creation of everything to Christ, saying *" All things were made through Him, and without Him nothing was made that was made." (John 1:3).* ✣

✣ And Paul says, concerning the divinity of the Lord and His incarnation: *"Beyond all question, the mystery of godliness is great: He appeared in a body. " (1 Tim. 3:16).*

✧   On this act of redemption which Christ performed, as God, Paul says to the people of   Ephesus: " *Therefore take heed to yourselves and to all the flock, among which the Holy Spirit has made you overseers, to shepherd the church of God which He purchased with His own blood.* " *(Acts 20:28)* Obviously it wouldn't have been possible for God to have 'bought' the Church by His blood, if He had not taken on a bodily form, and shed His blood on the cross.

St Thomas acknowledged Christ's divine nature when he put his finger into Christ's wounds after the Resurrection, and said to Him: *"My Lord and My God!" (John 20:28)*

The Lord Christ accepted from Thomas this believing in His divinity and scolded him for his doubts: *"Because you have seen Me, you have believed; blessed are those who have not seen and yet have believed" (John 20:29).*

Even the Lord's name was announced by an angel, as the Bible tells us: " *and they shall call His name Immanuel,*" *which is translated, "God with us."" (Matt. 1:23)*

This was fulfilment of the word of the prophet Isaiah that the Lord Himself would give us a sign: *"The Virgin shall conceive and bear a Son, and shall call His name Immanuel.* " *(Is. 7:14)*. God himself became a sign to the people through His birth by the Virgin Mary.

There are in fact many verses which attribute God's qualities to Christ.

[15]

IS THERE LIFE ON THE OTHER PLANETS?

Question

Scientists are interested in the question of whether there is life on the other planets. What would Christ's attitude to this subject be? And if science later confirms the existence of another form of life, would this have an effect on religion?

Answer:

Religion has left this subject without raising any arguments either for or against it. It makes no difference either way whether it is proved that there is life on the other planets or there isn't. If there is, it will have no effect on religion at all.

The Bible was not intended to be a book on the solar system, or a book of science, but the good news about salvation. It relates the story of salvation and all the history, commandments and theology connected with it.

As far as the stars are concerned, whatever might be on them has no connection with our salvation, it is enough that they give light to us at night, like a blessing from God to us. God likened His righteous saints to the stars, saying that they will shine like the lights in heaven.

Even if life were found on the other planets or the stars, there is nothing in the Bible that would be opposed to this, and vice versa.

[16]

REPLYING TO A QUESTION WITH A VERSE

Question

In the Seventh Day Adventists' book, 'God Speaks', there are questions on faith and belief, and each question is answered with a verse supporting it from the Bible.

Also, some leaflets which have come my way, have put forward certain teachings which the Church rejects, but which are backed up by verses from the gospels all the same. And because of this they claim that the teaching is the Gospel and Bible truth.

Why should we not believe what they say, since they confirm their doctrine with verses from the Bible?

Answer:

One verse from the Bible isn't sufficient and cannot be held to convey the total Biblical truth on a particular matter. This can only be gathered from collecting together all the verses which pertain to that subject.

I shall give you some examples to prove this point:

1. Let us suppose that a person asks you about being born of God, and how can man be born of God, and you put before him the following verse: " *If you know that He is righteous, you know that everyone who practices righteousness is born of Him.* " *(1 John 2:29).*

Is it possible by this verse alone to convey the whole Biblical teaching on this point, just by giving this brief statement that man is born of God through doing good works, without any mention of faith or baptism?

No, of course not. And all Christian denominations would say the same.

Alternatively, we could convey rather more of the Biblical truth on the subject of being born of God, by putting beside this verse the other verses which are also concerned with it, such as:

"I tell you the truth, no-one can enter the kingdom of God unless he is born of water and the Spirit. " (John 3:5)

"He saved us through the washing of rebirth and renewal by the Holy Spirit. " (Titus 3:5)

"He chose to give us birth through the word of truth. "(James 1:18)

2. Let's suppose someone asked you what was the religion that was acceptable to God. Would you only put before him

these words of James: "*Pure and undefiled religion before God and the Father is this: to visit orphans and widows in their trouble, and to keep oneself unspotted from the world*".*(James 1:27)*.

Can this be regarded as the whole biblical truth on this matter, when no mention is made in this verse of the need for faith? The other denominations wouldn't accept this! So let us provide for your questioner those other verses which together convey the full meaning of this point, which can then, when taken together, be regarded as biblical truth.

3   Again, let's imagine that a person asks you how a sinner can pass from death to eternal life. Would you reply to him simply be giving these words of John: "*We know that we have passed from death to life, because we love the brethren. He who does not love his brother abides in death.*" *(1 John 3:14)*.

Is this all that the Bible has to say on this matter, leaving out any mention of atonement, redemption and the blood of Christ, or of repentance and baptism?

No-one should accept this verse just by itself. We have to put beside it those other verses which concern this subject, such as:

"*God.. made us alive with Christ even when we were dead in transgressions.* " *(Eph. 2:5)*

"*When you were dead in your sins.. God made you alive with Christ. He forgave us all our sins, having cancelled the written code, with its regulations that was against us; he took it away, nailing it to the cross.* " *(Col. 2:13-14)*.

4. The same goes for the question of salvation, if you were to ask: 'How can I be saved?' The verse which says: " *Take heed to yourself and to the doctrine. Continue in them, for in doing this you will save both yourself and those who hear you.* " *(1 Tim. 4:16)*, might be put before you.

But is what it says in this verse alone enough for salvation, without faith and without baptism? And we could say the same for the verse: " *if you confess with your mouth the Lord Jesus and believe in your heart that God has raised Him from the dead, you will be saved.* " *Rom. 10:9)*

Why not add these following verses:

"*Whoever believes and is baptised will be saved.* " *(Mark 16:16)*

"*.. in the days of Noah while the ark was being built. In it only a few people, eight in all, were saved through water, and this water symbolises baptism that now saves you also (1 Pet. 3:20-21)*

By doing this, the whole biblical truth will be conveyed.

This question is one that constantly bewilders me, and I haven't yet found an answer to it:

Why don't those who call for the gospel teaching and who claim to defend biblical truth, state these verses which bring out the full meaning, in addition to those other ones? Aren't they all from the gospel and the Bible after all, I ask?!

[17]

QUESTIONS ABOUT THE HOLY SPIRIT

Question

I read in a book about Pentecost, that on the day of Pentecost, 'there was an invisible union between divine nature and human nature' and that, 'the divine nature was none other than the mystical body of Christ which preceded Christ and which He indicated was to be taken and eaten in order that we could be united with Him and abide in Him'.

What is your opinion on this supposed union with the divine nature? And what do you think of the following phrases, which I also read in that book: 'we are, therefore, like a burning bush', and 'the purpose of the divine incarnation was completed on the day of Pentecost', and 'the Church possesses all that was Christ's'?

Answer:

The Lord Christ is the only one who has a unity of the divine nature and the human nature. If this same union of the divine nature with the human were to happen to all believers, then what difference would there be between any human being and Christ?

There are two ways of attacking Christ's divinity: one is by belittling the importance of Christ and reducing Him to the level of ordinary human beings, as the Arians did, and the other is by raising people to the same level as Christ, which is referred to as defying the human being, in the kind of way that you have described in your question.

In both cases the outcome is the same: that Christ and human beings are placed on the same footing.

The Church cannot possess all that was Christ's, because the word 'all' would have to mean His divinity too. Christ gave the Church His love, but He did not, and does not, give His glory to another.

Theological terms always need to be used very precisely.

And what is this about a human being changed into a 'burning bush'? If that were to happen then the prophets would have to stand humbly before him to listen to the voice of God, just as Moses did *(Ex. 3)!* Human beings were not changed on the day of Pentecost into gods, and the divine incarnation which was Christ's alone, did not happen to them either.

As far as the phrase 'the divine nature was none other than the mystical body of Christ', is concerned, these are either the words of Eutyches, in which the dimension of Christ's humanity is lost, or they are supposed to mean that the divine nature was the same as the human, in which case there could be no divinity!

So what is this mystical body of Christ? Is it supposed to mean the Church?

The Church cannot be the divine nature. Nor can the Church be the body of Christ, which He instructed to be taken and eaten in the Eucharist. In the divine Mass we do not eat the Church! There is a confusion here between the body which Christ took from the Virgin Mary, and the Church when it is referred to as the 'body' of Christ.

Is this body, the body which in the sacrament of the Eucharist the Lord instructed us to take and eat? If this were so, this body could not be the divine nature, otherwise we would be going back to the ideas of Eutyches! We say in the Liturgy, "This is the life-giving body which Your Only Son received from our lady and Queen of us all the pure St Mary.. and He made it one with His divinity."

Here too, an important question stands out, which is: were the words spoken on the day of Pentecost about the third person of the Holy Trinity (ie. the Holy Spirit), or the second, namely the Son, who was incarnated for our sake, and who said: "Take, eat, this is My body"? And what has the sacrament of the Eucharist got to do with the day of Pentecost on which the Holy Spirit descended like tongues of fire?

In your question there still remain some points which need to be explained:

a) Was what happened on the day of Pentecost, a descent or a union? The Bible speaks unequivocally about the descent of the Holy Spirit. And the Lord Jesus Christ said: *"you will receive power when the Holy Spirit comes on you. " (Acts 1:8)*

b)   Was the burning bush a symbol of the divine incarnation, or was it a symbol of the day of Pentecost? And was the nature, purpose and results of what happened in the divine incarnation, what the disciples experienced on the day of Pentecost, such that one could say that the purpose behind the divine incarnation had reached its peak on the day of Pentecost?

c)   And did the third Person of the Holy Trinity become incarnated in mankind on the day of Pentecost, by descending upon those present, or uniting with them, according to what you have read?

[18]

WAS THE HOLY SPIRIT THE ANGEL GABRIEL?

Question

I heard someone say that the Holy Spirit was the angel Gabriel. Is this true? And some people say that it is the spirit of a prophet. Could this be true?

Answer:

The Holy Spirit is the Spirit of God, not the spirit of an angel or prophet. For if it were that of an angel or prophet, it would be restricted, whereas the Holy Spirit, according to what the gospel tells us is unbounded.

If the Holy Spirit descends upon all believers, as the Bible says: " *Or do you not know that your body is the temple of the Holy Spirit who is in you, whom you have from God, and you are not your own?" (1 Cor. 6.19)*, would it be reasonable to suppose that an angel or prophet could descend on all believing humans in their hundreds and thousands?

In the Bible it also says, concerning the martyrs: " *"But when they deliver you up, do not worry about how or what you should speak. For it will be given to you in that hour what you should speak; for it is not you who speak, but the Spirit of your Father who speaks in you. " (Matt. 10:19-20)*

Would it have been possible for an angel or prophet to speak through the mouths of the thousands of martyrs at the beginning of the Christian era, who bore witness to Christ in so many different and far-flung places at the same time?

Referring to the Holy Spirit, the Lord Christ said: *"the Father ... will give you another Helper, that He may abide with you forever; the Spirit of truth, whom the world cannot receive, because it neither sees Him nor knows Him; but you know Him, for He dwells with you and will be in you." (John 14:16-17)* Obviously these words could not have been referring to a prophet, because a prophet could not be with men for ever, and also because people would have been able to see him and recognise him. Likewise it could not be meant to apply to an angel, because an angel could not stay with all believers for ever and ever, because he is not boundless.

The Bible goes on to say: *"But you know Him, for He dwells with you and will be in you." (John 14:17)* So who could this 'angel' or 'prophet' be who stays with all people and is in them for ever?

The Lord Jesus Christ was the Good Teacher, who brought the true teaching to mankind, and opened men's hearts and minds to the highest principles of all, so that they were amazed at His teaching.

As far as Adam was concerned, the Bible does not record that there was any teaching or spiritual guidance for his generation, or even for his kinsfolk, for Adam gave in to his wife's mistaken direction. Christ has always been the head.

It was Christ who redeemed Adam and his sons, and freed them from the penalty of sin, who died for them and their descendants, and who bought them with His blood.

So Christ was the Redeemer, and Adam and his sons, the redeemed.

All this is seen from the human point of view, but from the theological standpoint the matter is too extensive to be written about in a brief answer to a question like this, which is just one of many being answered.

[19]

WHY ARE THERE SEVEN MYSTERIES OR (SACRAMENTS)?

Question

The word secret, mystery or sacrament occurs a number of times in the Bible, as when for example the apostle Paul says: *"Beyond all question, the mystery of godliness is great: He appeared in a body" (1 Tim. 3:16),* and *"the mystery of the gospel. " (Eph. 6:19) and "the secret Power of lawlessness. " (2 Thess. 2:7)* and so on. Why are there Seven Sacraments?

Answer:

The word "sacrament" or mystery when used in the Church is not used just in the way that the dictionary defines it, but is a technical term with a specific meaning of its own.

Each of the Church's mysteries or sacraments consists of a mysterious divine blessing which you cannot see, but which you receive in secret from the Holy Spirit through the prayers which a legitimate priest offers up in a special ritual, along

With the presence of a specific substance, which is the material of the sacrament or mystery.

It is not a mystery or sacrament in the sense of being something recognisable, such as when the Bible says: *"the mystery of the seven stars"* *(Rev. 1:20)*

A sacrament is conditional upon four elements which are: sacramental grace, a priest, prayers and ritual and the substance of the sacrament.

In baptism, for example, there exists something mysterious that is unseen, which is the new birth through water and the Spirit *(John 3:5)*. Or you might say that in baptism you are being *"clothed.. with Christ. "* *(Gal. 3:27)*, or that you *"wash your sins away"* *(Acts 22:16)* or that you are buried with Christ and die with Him *(Rom. 6)*.

These heavenly blessings are a mysterious action which the Holy Spirit performs in the human being, through the priest's special prayers, and a special ritual which involves the one being baptised, being submerged in water three times. So here, then, the substance of the mystery is the water.

The mysterious blessing in the Chrism (the Myron) is the descent of the Holy Spirit, and in the sacrament of confession it is the wiping away of sins by the blood of Christ, and in the Eucharist it is the transformation of bread and wine into the body and blood of the Lord, while in marriage it is the joining together of the two into one etc.
None of these blessings can be seen by the human eye, therefore they are a mystery.

They are things that cannot be distinguished by intellectual knowledge, like mysteries pertaining to ultimately knowable facts, data, learning or information, but are spiritual elements to do with faith which go beyond what can be expressed in words.

The Church has defined these mysterious blessings to be seven in number, and has prescribed special prayers for them and the rituals which they require.

There are, of course, other prayers and rituals which are not to do with the sacraments, such as the prayer for the departed, which isn't a sacrament but just simply a prayer, a request, in which the Church asks for compassion for the souls of those passing on.

And here *"The knowledge of the secrets of the kingdom of heaven. " (Matt. 13:11),* which are boundless, we now see as but *"a poor reflection as in a mirror" (1 Cor. 13:12),* but God will bring them to our knowledge in due time. These are not, however, part of the mysterious gifts which the believer receives on earth, and which the Church is engaged in giving to him by virtue of the authority granted to it by God.

So there is no need for anyone to confuse one kind of mystery with another.

Mysteries to do with things that are knowable, are quite different from mysteries in the sense of the sacraments which pertain to heavenly grace.

[20]

ARE THE SACRAMENTS NECESSARY FOR ALL PEOPLE?

Question

Are the Church's Seven Sacraments necessary for all people?

Answer:

Baptism is necessary for everyone because, " *He who believes and is baptised will be saved* " *(Mark 16:16)*, and without it no-one can enter the kingdom of heaven *(John 3:5)*.

The bestowing of the Holy Spirit in the sacrament of the holy anointing is necessary for all. And the Church has been doing this for all believers since the time of the apostles *(Acts 8)*.

Similarly, the sacrament of repentance is necessary for all people, because nobody is without sin.

Also the Eucharist is an essential sacrament for everyone, since the Lord says: *"unless you can eat the flesh of the Son of Man and drink His blood, you have no life in you. " (John 6:53)*

The sacrament of the priesthood also has a bearing on all people. It does not only apply to those who are ordained as priests, but is relevant to all believers in that they receive the blessings of all the seven sacraments by way of the priest, whom we call the 'servant of the mysteries'.

We could talk about the sacrament of marriage for example, though it is clear that some people do not need this sacrament themselves, since they live without partners. Nevertheless, even those who are celibate are the fruit of the union of man and woman.

So the sacrament of marriage and that of priesthood, although not practised by all people, are notwithstanding of benefit to all, and they are essential to the Church as a whole.

The sacrament of anointing the sick is necessary for the sick only, and if a person never receives it, perhaps because he has never needed it, this obviously will not affect his salvation.

[21]

IS THE SACRAMENT STILL THE SAME WHEN A SHORTENED SERVICE IS USED?

Question

Sometimes we attend a long Mass and sometimes a shorter version, and it seems that baptism can take an hour or just a few minutes. Is the sacrament still being performed properly even though the ceremony is shorter?

Answer:

As far as baptism is concerned, it consists of two parts. The first of which is the blessing of the baptismal water, which is a long ceremony, and can take an hour to perform. The second part, is the actual baptism of the child or adult, which may take only a few minutes.

What happens is that the priest might pray over the water very early on, before the arrival of those in the baptism party, so because they have not attended this part of the ritual they might think that the baptism has just taken a few minutes to perform, whereas if they had been present from the very beginning, it would have taken more than an hour. Therefore what you imagined to be shorter version of the ceremony was in fact a part of the full-length baptism ritual.

As far as the Mass is concerned, though, there are prayers which are fundamental to the consecration of the Host, such as the signing with the cross, Christ's covenant with us, the invocation of the Holy Spirit, the division and distribution, and the final confession. But the intercessions, for instance, and the commemoration of the saints, the sermon and the various readings are not connected with the actual consecration of the sacrament, but are nevertheless recited as part of the liturgy of the Mass, which is after all the holiest of the services in the Church.

In the time of the martyrs, during the persecution of the Church, the Mass was abridged without any damage being done to the sacrament. Also one can shorten it by abbreviating or eliminating some of the chants, for the music isn't part of the consecration of the sacrament but serves to deepen the spirit of prayer. So don't be apprehensive or suspicious about the validity of the shorter Mass, because the sacrament is still being fully carried out.

[22]

THE POINT OF TRANSUBSTANTIATION IN THE SACRAMENT OF THE EUCHARIST

Question

When do the bread and wine change into the body and blood of the Lord in the Sacrament of the Eucharist?

I have read one of the Fathers who said that the transformation of the bread and wine takes place in the Eucharist when the sign of the cross is first made over them at the offering of the Host, and that this is what has happened since early times.

Answer:

The transubstantiation of the holy mysteries takes place when the Holy Spirit descends, and not before.

And the descent of the Holy Spirit takes place just before the Intercessions and the commemoration of the saints. So the priest prays in secret saying: "Let Your Holy Spirit descend upon us and upon these sacrifices placed here. Purify them and transform them and make them to appear holy to your saints ".

Then he makes the sign of the cross over the bread three times and calls aloud: 'He makes this bread His holy body'. Then he makes the sign of the cross three times over the chalice and, calls aloud: '.. and this cup too, He makes the honoured blood of the New Testament...' and the people say 'Amen' after both of these.

This proves that no transformation takes place during the offering of the Host.

For if the mysteries were transformed before this point, the priest would not call for the Holy Spirit to descend to change them.

We also observe that after the descent of the Holy Spirit to transform the sacraments, the priest does not make the sign of the cross, and does not look behind him.

Before that - after the offering of the Host and the signing of the cross - the priest makes the sign of the cross over the people, and the bread and wine. However, after its transubstantiation, when the Holy Spirit has descended, he does not make the sign of the cross over the people any more, not even when he says, 'Peace be with you all'. In fact he just bows his head without signing the cross.

Nor does he sign the cross over the chalice or the offertory paten (tray), but makes the sign of the cross with each of the sacraments in turn, after their transubstantiation, over the other one.

This means that the blood is crossed by the body, and the body by the blood, but the priest doesn't do it with his hand or finger at all.

He does not turn round to face the people at all when he blesses them but instead focuses his concentration on the holy mysteries, without turning away from them.

From this one can see that to say that the mysteries are transformed directly after the offering of the Host during the first signing of the cross, is inaccurate. If it were so, then it would mean that the mysteries are sanctified and transformed, during the part of the Mass that is attended by the catechumens for those are not allowed to attend the whole Mass.

But we observe that in the early days of the Church, the catechumens used to attend the offering of the Host and the reading of the epistles and the gospel and the sermon, and would then depart. And the deacon, before the raising of the holy veil concealing the sacraments, meaning before the Holy Mass was begun, would say: 'Let no-one who is unconfirmed or who is an unbeliever stand here, but let only those believers stay who are worthy to attend the divine Mass'. (See the canons of the apostles and those of Apolides.)

Studying the history of the Church's ceremonies calls for a knowledge of theology of the rituals involved and also their spirituality.

Since history does not conflict with theology, we can see that it cannot be said that in the past, the holy mysteries used to be transformed from the bread and wine into the body and blood of the Lord, before the descent of the Holy Spirit upon them and the prayers of the priest invoking this descent.

[23]

ABOUT THE PRAYER OF "THE UNCTION OF THE SICK" BEING SAID IN HOMES

Question

Is it proper for the Prayer of the "Unction of the Sick " to he said in homes during a fast, even if there isn't someone ill there?

For it has been noticed that the Church Fathers and many individuals from among the congregation have been used to doing this, is it right to continue this practice or should it be abolished?

Answer:

The Prayer of the "Unction of the Sick " known by the name "The Lamp Prayer" is essentially, and above all, a prayer on behalf of the sick, and their anointing with oil, but it also has many benefits.

1.   It is an opportunity for meeting together in the home, and of blessing the home by prayer, and of raising up incense. It is a chance for the Father Priest to visit and read the Absolution, and pray for all those in the home. All these

benefits are in any case irrespective of the kind of prayer that is said and its purpose.

2. The Prayer of the "Unction of the Sick" includes many other prayers, such as the Lord's Prayer, the Thanksgiving, the Trisagion and the Kyries, along with a number of other prayers asking for God's mercy, all of which are beneficial.

3. The Prayer of the "Unction of the Sick " comprises all the main intercessions which are offered to God with the raising of the incense, including those for the sick and the departed for the travellers and for those who are awaiting baptism and confirmation, as well as prayers for the Church, for its meetings, for those who offer its sacrifices, and the heads of state etc. So everyone who attends this finds his situation is included in it somewhere.

4. The Prayer of the "Unction of the Sick" also contains prayers calling for individual repentance and asking for God's mercies. And we ask Him to accept us just as He accepted the woman who was a sinner, and Zacchaeus the tax collector, and to pardon us just as He forgave the debtor. Anyone, even if he is in perfect health, will undoubtedly benefit from these humbling, contrite prayers, and will be led to repentance through them, if he follows them with an open heart.

5. It also includes the reading of at least seven chapters from the gospels, chosen for their particular wisdom. And simply listening to the Bible being read aloud in the home a number of times is something beneficial.

6.   Let us not forget the holy rituals in these prayers, like the incense and the candles, the oil and the hymn, all of which are of great benefit, even to children who might not understand them all , and they make everyone feel that the home has become a part of the Church.

7.   Because of this, we feel that it is right to continue this custom of saying the Prayer of the "Unction of the Sick" in people's homes, even if there is no-one there who is ill, for anyone of us might have a hidden illness which we don't know about, and there are always psychological and spiritual imbalances which we might have but may not recognise.

[24]

THE NUMBER OF HEAVENS

Question

I heard that there are only three heavens, because the Holy Bible says Everything is perfected in the number three.

Answer:

I would like to say to the one who sent in this phrase that there is no verse in the Bible which says that! This is purely a worldly expression! Perfection isn't confined to the number three. Number seven, for example, is sometimes made a symbol for perfection and so is ten etc.

The expression 'the third heaven' comes in the Bible as a name for Paradise *(2 Cor. 12:2,4)*. But reference to the heaven which is the throne of God comes in *John 3:13 and Matt. 5:34*. On the other hand, the *'highest heavens'* mentioned in *Psalm 148:4*, must obviously be higher than the third. This is the heaven to which only the Lord Jesus Christ has ascended, and to which no human being will ever rise. *(John 3:13)*.

[25]

CAN SATAN ENTER A CHURCH?

Question

Is it possible for Satan to enter a church, one which has been consecrated? And if he can, how could this be so, since the church is supposed to be full of angels, and also to contain the Holy Spirit?

Answer:

We remember in the story of the righteous Job, that the Bible said: *"One day the angels came to present themselves before the Lord, and Satan also came with them. The Lord said to Satan, 'Where have You come from?'"* *(Job. 1:6-7)*. And Satan plotted against Job.

So Satan was able to dare to stand in a holy place where God Himself stood, in order to try and cause to one of God's believers harm.

We read how Satan came to the Lord Christ on the mountain and dared to tempt Him, using verses from the Bible, and what is more, he also stood with the Lord Christ on the pinnacle of the temple to put Him to the test there.

But of course that was all with the Lord's permission.

We hear in the Old Testament of sins that were committed in holy places, in the days of Eli the priest, by his sons which provoked God's anger. No doubt these were caused by Satan's intervention.

Satan might enter a church to distract the thoughts of the believers, to take their minds off of the prayers, out of envy that they are worshipping God.

And although some believers might defeat him by the strength of their prayers, others may be weakened. Whether a church has been consecrated isn't really the issue, because it depends on whether the individual believer has been consecrated, through being anointed with oil at baptism. Nevertheless, Satan can still enter his heart and thoughts to test him.

God may give Satan freedom to act, but it would be freedom within a limited sphere, and he would be judged for it.

So we say that Satan nowadays is fettered, and has been since the Crucifixion. And if Satan is fettered it means that he isn't totally free, otherwise he would have destroyed the world by now!

There have been times when the Lord has said: 'Go away Satan!', as happened at the temptation on the mountain, or when He has set him limits which he cannot exceed, such as in Job's temptation.

I am pretty sure that most of all Satan cannot bear the moment when the Holy Spirit descends and the sacraments are transformed during the divine Mass.

He cannot bear these holy moments, and God does not permit him to act then. Also, at this point, the believers are usually in an elevated spiritual state in which it is likely for them to respond to distracting ideas from Satan who at that moment is troubled by the deep heartfelt humility of the believers, and the action of the Spirit upon the sacraments and the congregation.

Generally speaking, if Satan enters a church in order to do something then he is in a weak position. And he cannot find real scope to act there except within the people who are inside the church, but whose hearts and minds are outside the Church!

Satan may try to cast doubts in people's minds, even on holy occasions and during prayers, but since the people's hearts are connected to God, any doubts that they might have remain outside them, however heavy and forceful they might be, and thus Satan has to depart unsuccessful.

[26]

FASTING AND EATING FISH

Question

Why don't we eat fish on Wednesdays and Fridays but during some other fasts, in view of the fact, so I have heard, that in olden times they used to eat fish on Wednesdays and Fridays?

Answer:

Some believers in the past used to eat fish on Wednesdays and Fridays, and this was undoubtedly on account either a mistaken understanding of the Church's teaching on their part, or because it was a wrong habit which they had inherited or had passed down to them from others who had been mistaken.

Our kind of fasting in the Orthodox Church is eating vegan foods. As everyone knows, we abstain from meat and all foodstuff of animal origin during fasting days. Obviously fish are included as flesh foods, so to eat fish is not in accordance with our kind of fasting at all. So you mustn't be surprised at the non-eating of fish on the fasting days of Wednesday and Friday.

In fact you should really be surprised at eating fish during a vegan fast!
The general rule is not to eat fish during the fasts.

However, since there are so many fasts in the Coptic Church, around two hundred days in the year, which means more than half a year in fasting, the eating of fish during certain fasts, which are of the minor order, is permitted as a way of reducing the lengthy period of the fast for the people.

But eating fish is not allowed during major fasts or on Wednesdays and Fridays because these are counted among the major fasts.

The most important of these major fasts is the period of the forty holy days which the Lord fasted, and Pascha Week, the week of His suffering. On Wednesdays we remember how He was betrayed and plotted against, and on Fridays we recall His crucifixion.

People can eat meat all the days of the week, except Wednesdays and Fridays. So if they were to eat fish on those days, the result would be the consumption of fish foods every day of the week, since fish is included in this category! And it wouldn't be right to make things that easy.

It wouldn't be very logical either, if we were to remember Christ's betrayal and crucifixion by eating fish! We'd be letting ourselves off rather lightly! This remembrance demands a greater degree of renunciation and devotion than that.

On another occasion some asked **whether fish could he eaten on the Day of Our Lady, the festival of the Annunciation, which is one of the Lord's festivals.** The Day of Our Lady is of course the 29th Baramhat (the seventh Coptic month), and always comes during the lent. So the answer to this question is that the lent takes precedence and shouldn't be broken under any circumstances, even on account of the Annunciation, because it is still part of the Lord's fast.

To break the fast on this occasion would show a lack of self-control. How could anyone fast for more than a month of the lent and then let himself be tempted by a piece of fish during the fast on the Day of Annunciation? What would that say about one's efforts towards trying to rise above the level of material things and not indulge oneself in scrumptious foods?!

[27]

THE ASCENT INTO HEAVEN AND THE EARTH'S GRAVITY

Question

When the Lord rose to heaven, did He break the law of the earth's gravity?

Answer:

To answer this question let us recall two points which are:

1.   That God set down the laws of Nature, in the first place, so that Nature would submit to him, and not He to them.

2.   That material or physical things on earth submit to the law of gravity, whereas the Lord Christ, when He ascended, did not do so in a physical body or an earthly one, which would have been subject to the laws of gravity.

The Lord's body of the Resurrection and the Ascension was a glorious body, a spiritual and heavenly one. If we too are to rise with such bodies, according to what it says in *1 Corinthians 15:43-50*, it goes without saying that our Lord would have such a body, and an even better one. And we are told that Christ, *"will transform our lowly bodies so that they will be like His glorious body. " (Phil. 3:21)*

This glorious body, in which our Lord rose from the dead and ascended, was therefore not subject to the earthly laws of gravity. And this brings us face to face with an important question:

Was there, then, nothing miraculous in His ascension?

Of course it was a miracle. But it wasn't contrary to the earth's law of gravity.

The miracle was in the transformation of the physical body into a spiritual, heavenly body that could rise up.

So the Ascension was not something contrary to Nature, but rather an elevation of the natural state of Christ's body which rose to heaven. It was a kind of manifestation of this nature.

And just as the Lord granted us to be in His form and likeness when He created us *(Gen. 1:26-27),* so shall we also be in His form and likeness at the Resurrection and Ascension.

This will all happen to us when we are glorified with Him and rise with Him in glory.

When we rise in power and glory, those living on earth at the time of the Resurrection will be changed: " *in a flash, in the twinkling of an eye, at the last trumpet. For the trumpet will sound, the dead will be raised incorruptible."* (1 Cor. 15:52-53) *" Then we who are alive and remain shall be caught up together with them in the clouds to meet the Lord in the air. And thus we shall always be with the Lord."* (1 Thess. 4:17)

[28]

WHY THE CROSS?

Question

Why did Christ have to die on the cross and not some other way?

Answer:

Death on the cross was considered shameful, so the Lord chose the kind of death that was the most shameful and most horrible at that time. This is why Paul says in *Hebrews 12:2* that the Lord, *"endured the cross, scorning its shame. "* So there was humiliation on the cross, and because of this Paul said: *"Let us go forth to Him, outside the camp, bearing His reproach. "* *(Heb. 13.13),* for the cross was considered a disgrace.

In the Old Testament, the cross was considered a curse, and it was said that whoever was hung upon a cross was accursed. The Lord intended by His crucifixion to bear all the curses which could fall on mankind, which the Law indicated *(Deut. 28),* so that He could give us a blessing, and so that there should be no more curses in the future.

The cross was considered *"foolishness"* by the Jews *(1 Cor. 1:18),* so Christ chose this disgrace and changed the cross into a sign of strength.

Crucifixion on the cross was also one of the most painful ways to die, since it tore the tissues of the body in a most excruciating way, besides draining the body of its fluids through bleeding. So by His crucifixion Christ suffered the worst pains that mankind could ever be crushed by.

Crucifixion was a manner of death in which the person who was to die was literally raised above the earth, so Jesus could say that after He had been 'raised' above the earth He would draw all men to Himself. Just as the Lord Christ was raised on the cross, so was He raised in glory in His ascension. By His crucifixion He has also raised us with Him, from the level of dust and earth.

In His death Christ stretched out His arms to all mankind, in a gesture of His acceptance. of all people.

[29]

GOD'S JUSTICE AND MERCY

Question

I read this question in a book: Was what happened on the cross the reconciliation of God's justice with His mercy?

Answer:

There has never been any conflict between God's justice and His mercy, because there cannot be any contradiction between the qualities of God. God is merciful in His justice and just in His mercy.

The justice of God is full of mercy. The mercy of God is full of justice. We can say that God's justice is a merciful justice and that His mercy is a just mercy. We cannot separate at all God's mercy from His justice.

When we speak on one occasion of justice, and on another of mercy, we are not talking of two different things but of varying aspects of the same thing.

Meimar al-Abd al-Maimluk (a special reading during the Good Friday) imagined a dispute and an argument between God's justice and mercy, which is a kind of theological debate, but it is not correct from the theological point of view, and there have been many objections to it. For naturally such a disagreement never took place. The author of the Meimar, however, wanted to point out the details of the subject in the form of a discussion. This is a style that sometimes makes for interesting reading, but it is not a theologically accurate one.

On the cross, however, as the psalm tells us, justice and mercy join together, or mercy and truth join together (not that they are reconciled!).

The word 'reconciliation' implies the existence of an opposition, and heaven forbid that there should ever be or have been, anything so at odds among the attributes of God!

Even the expression 'join together' means a joining together before us, in our presence, and is conditioned by our concept of this process, while from the theological standpoint, mercy and justice have been joined together in harmony right from eternity. It is as we have said, that God's mercy is full of justice and His justice is full of mercy.

It was on the cross that we saw this union between justice and mercy and it is indeed a permanent union. But we, being human beings, only perceived it when it was brought to our attention on the cross. That was when we saw this beautiful image, which gave to our human minds an understanding that mercy and justice were combined. ✟

[30]

ABOUT BEING RE-BAPTISED

Question

Is it possible to be re-baptised? Is baptism ever done twice?

Don't we say in the Creed, "We believe in one baptism for the forgiveness of sins"? And doesn't the Bible say that there is "*one baptism*" ? *(Eph. 4.5)*.

Answer:

Yes, the Bible says that there is "*one baptism*", but please let us read a bit more of the verse, which tells us that there is "one faith" and "one baptism".

For wherever one faith exists, one baptism is found too.

Therefore we don't re-baptise a person who has been baptised in a church which shares our Orthodox faith.

Also, baptism must be performed by a properly qualified priest who has full priestly authority to carry out the holy sacrament of baptism, and who believes totally in the effective action of this sacrament.

For example, the churches which do not believe in the sacrament of the priesthood and which do not have priests and do not believe that baptism is a sacrament, do not share our belief in the effectiveness of baptism, so we can't really accept their baptism.

The same applies to churches which believe in the sacrament of baptism and its effectiveness and in the sacrament of the priesthood, but are closed to us according to anathemas set by the Fathers.

These anathemas must be removed first, then their church sacraments would be acceptable to us.

[31]

IS THERE A THIRD PLACE FOR WORSHIPPING GOD?

Question

The Lord Jesus Christ said to the Samaritan woman: " *the hour is coming when you will neither on this mountain, nor in Jerusalem, worship the Father."* *(John 4:21)* **Does this sentence carry a prophecy about there being a specific third place, besides these two, where God is to he worshipped, because I have heard from some people that this is so?**

Answer:

The Jews thought it right that God should be worshipped in the Temple in Jerusalem, because this was the only holy place in which sacrifices were offered. They didn't believe that other people could have different holy places, and they applied that especially to the Samaritans because of the enmity which existed between them and the Jews.

The Samaritans however had their own holy mountain.

When the Lord Christ spoke these words to the Samaritan woman, he was not alluding to a third place, and was not defining an alternative spot either, but was referring to the spread of the faith to the Gentiles.

That is, He was not singling out Jerusalem alone or Samaria as being places of worship, but was saying that faith was for all peoples and nations, and that worship could be performed in any sacred place on earth, but *"the true worshippers will worship the Father in spirit and truth." (John 4:23)*

The Lord Christ was not substituting one nation for another, but was in fact opening the door to all.

If He had meant that there was a third place, then it would have meant that the concept of God's 'chosen people' was to remain (and just apply to the Jews), but that it simply moved from one place to another, and that there was to be no general diffusion of the religion. This, of course, would have been at odds with what He said to His holy disciples: " *Go into all the world and preach the gospel to every creature." (Mark 16:15),* and " *Go therefore and make disciples of all the nations, " (Matt. 28:19),* also, *"you shall be My witnesses in Jerusalem, and in all Judea and Samaria, and to the ends of the earth. " (Acts 1:8)*

Yet the Lord Christ did not declare that Jerusalem was not to be considered holy, nor did He substitute some other place for it. The people of the whole world till this day go to Jerusalem and worship there.

The true worshippers of God are those who worship Him in spirit and in truth. And this was what Jesus meant by His words to the Samaritan woman, who considered that the hostility between the Jews and the Samaritans, and their different places of worship, were a barrier to her faith.

The place where worship is performed is not the most important thing, but what is important is that the person worships in spirit and truth, wherever he may be.

The true worshippers are those who worship God in spirit and truth, for they are the kind of worshippers the Father seeks. *"God is Spirit and those who worship Him must worship in spirit and truth." (John 4:23-24).*

So where is this 'third' place then? There is no indication, or definition or prophecy concerning it. It is rather an explanation of the true meaning of worship, and of not restricting it to a particular location.

[32]

HAS SATAN BEEN RELEASED FROM HIS PRISON AND IS THE LAST DAY APPROACHING?

Question

I read in a newspaper that someone was saying that Satan had been freed from his prison in 1967, and that we were approaching the last day. What do you think?

Answer:

Why did the author of that article choose the year 1967 rather than another?

What basis is there in the Bible to support that? Upon what calculation was it made?

Many people in the past have defined dates for what they believed would be the end of the world, and probably the Jehovah's Witnesses have been most prominent in doing this. They said that Christ would come to rule in 1914, but the date came, and Christ didn't! The Seventh Day Adventists and the Plymouth Brethren have also foretold the end of the world, and have challenged the word of the Bible in a startling way

According to what Jesus Christ Himself said to His holy disciples:

" It is not for you to know times or seasons which the Father has put in His own authority." (Acts 1:7)

According to St Paul: *"Do not think of yourself more highly than you ought. " (Rom. 12:3)* So why do some people take it upon themselves to decide things that are way above their level, and beyond their human understanding? These things are under the authority of the Father alone. But let us look now at what will happen when Satan is freed from his prison. The Bible says:

" Now when the thousand years have expired, Satan will be released from his prison and will go out to deceive the nations which are in the four corners of the earth, " (Rev. 20.7-8)

So, had a thousand years passed when we got to 1967? And if so, from when and how did they calculate it?

Is Satan, therefore, now that we are some twenty odd years past that date (1967), able to lead the nations astray?

The Lord said: " *And unless those days were shortened, no flesh would be saved; but for the elect's sake those days will be shortened .... For false christs and false prophets will rise and show great signs and wonders to deceive, if possible, even the elect." (Matt. 24:22-24)* Has any of that happened yet? For if Satan had been set free from his prison, he would be trying with all his might to bring this about, knowing that he would have an easy time. *(Rev. 20:3)*

The choice of 1967, then, was not a very satisfactory one after all!

In fact for us in Egypt, 1967 was rather a good year, for it was in that year that the foundations were laid of the main cathedral, which was opened the following year. And on 2nd April 1968, St Mary appeared in Zeitun, and a great spiritual revival took place as a result of this appearance and its miracles. Could all this have happened if Satan had been released from his prison?

On the world stage, during these past few years, after which the supposed prophecy claimed that Satan had been freed, we have seen President Gorbachov begin a policy of freedom of conscience, and the revival of the Church in Russia. America and Russia have agreed on the elimination of medium-range nuclear weapons, and the nations of the world are now moving towards abolishing chemical weapons and other destructive weapons. Could all of this be happening if Satan had been released from his prison?

When Satan was free in olden times, he was able to bring down all the nations of the world to worship idols, so that paganism and primitive forms of worship were widespread.

Only the Jews remained worshipping God, and later they too fell into paganism.

When Moses was detained on the holy mountain talking with God, and the tribe of Israel worshipped the golden calf, who was worshipping God then? There were only two people, Moses and Joshua.

Those days when Satan is released from his prison to lead the nations astray will be terrifying, unless God limits them, for otherwise no one would saved.

We could hardly be living in those days now, with churches filled with worshippers and hundreds and thousands of people receiving Holy Communion in every church each week!

When Satan is released, false prophets and false Messiahs will abound, according to what Christ said, and they will, " *will rise and show great signs and wonders to deceive, if possible, even the elect.* " *(Matt. 24:24)* So where are these people and their miracles today?

There are many signs which will herald the last days, none of which have yet taken place.

What about the 'Antichrist', who according to St Paul will oppose and exalt himself over everything that is called God or is worshipped, so that he sits as God in the temple of God, showing himself that he is God." *(2 Thess. 2:4)* and " *The coming of the lawless one is according to the working of Satan, with all power, signs, and lying wonders, and with all unrighteous deception among those who perish, ...*"? *(2 Thess. 2:9)*

And what about the apostasy of the world, which is supposed to follow the coming of the Antichrist and his miracles?

What about the prophecies of Enoch and Elijah?

What about the faith of the Jews? *(Rom. 11:26)* And what about the words; *"And they will fall by the edge of the sword, ... until the times of the Gentiles are fulfilled. " (Luke 21:24),* and *" until the fullness of the Gentiles has come in." (Rom. 11:25)?*

The final signs will be the destruction of Nature.

The Lord said: *"Immediately after the tribulation of those days the sun will be darkened, and the moon will not give its light; the stars will fall from heaven, and the powers of the heavens will be shaken.". (Matt. 24:29)*

So, theological matters really call for humility of heart.

We cannot claim to know everything. If we are asked about subjects like the date of Satan's release from his prison, and the end of time, which we cannot answer, we should simply say without embarrassment that we do not know, and not try to claim that we do know, or think of ourselves more highly than we should!

The Bible says that Satan will he bound for a thousand years, and that when that period has passed, he will he freed from his prison. How, then, could that thousand years have been completed by the year 1967, by any calculation, whether literally or symbolically?

This is a very serious point: if an idea occurs to us, we shouldn't just present it to people as doctrine! *"He who has ears to hear, let him hear!"(Matt. 13:9)* ✣

[33]

WHO ARE THE SEVENTH-DAY ADVENTISTS?

Question

Who are the Seventh Day Adventists?

Answer :

The Adventists are a dangerous heretical sect which shares with the Jehovah's Witnesses many serious errors. Among the most well-known of their heretical beliefs are:

1. They believe that Christ is the angel Michael.

2. They believe that Christ was born in original sin.

3. They call the Holy Spirit, 'the vice-regent of the Lord's host'.

4. They believe that Saturday is the Lord's day, instead of Sunday.

5. They don't believe in the immortality of the soul.

6. They believe that Jesus will come three times in all.
7. They believe in an earthly kingdom and that heaven will not be for mankind.

8. They believe in the extinction of the wicked and not their torture.

9. They don't believe in the priesthood or intercession, or most of the other sacraments of the Church.

10. They have many other wrong beliefs which I will point out later, if God wills.

In addition to this, they have a Protestant origin, which means they deny the passing on of tradition, and the reverence of the saints, and do not use candles, incense or an altar, and do not share our Church's rituals, and refuse the Church canons, councils, the Fathers and the priesthood.

I am hoping that by God's grace I will be able to bring out a book about them for you, in which I can repudiate their beliefs, and especially what their leader, Alan White, has said in their books.

[34]

WAS THE USE OF INCENSE ABOLISHED IN THE NEW TESTAMENT?

Question

Some people say that incense was used to get rid of the smell of blood during the sacrifices in the Old Testament, so that when the blood sacrifices were abolished in the New Testament, the use of incense was consequently abolished. Is this true?

Answer:

This is not true. The offering of incense was something on its own, which the priest could do without performing a sacrifice.

When God struck the tribe of Israel with the plague, Moses ordered Aaron, the chief priest, to raise the incense and to stand between the living and the dead. And on account of the offering of incense, God accepted their intercession and put an end to the plague. *(Num. 16..48)* On this occasion no sacrifice was made, and there was no smell of blood to be disguised. Incense was just used alone.

There was also a separate altar called 'the altar of incense' *(Ex. 30. 1)*, which Aaron lit each morning and evening so that there would always be incense before the Lord, and this had no connection with the sacrifices.

The incense was considered a sacrifice on its own. Thus the place where it was offered was called 'the altar of incense'.

We read of the priest Zechariah when the angel announced to him that Elizabeth would give birth to John the Baptist that: *"when Zechariah's division was on duty and he was serving as priest before God, he was chosen by lot, according to the custom of the priesthood, to go into the temple of the Lord and burn incense. " (Luke 1:8)* and *"an angel of the Lord appeared to him, standing at the right side of the altar of incense." (Luke 1:11)*

So incense on its own could constitute a sacrifice, and there didn't have to be a blood sacrifice which would need to have its smell taken away by any incense.

We observe the same in the New Testament in the Book of Revelation.

There is an angel who offers a lot of incense with the prayers of the saints: " *Then another angel, having a golden censer, came and stood at the altar. He was given much incense, that he should offer it with the prayers of all the saints upon the golden altar which was before the throne. And the smoke of the incense, with the prayers of the saints, ascended before God from the angel's hand.. " (Rev. 8:3-4)* There were no blood sacrifices involved. There was also the incense offered by the twenty four elders *(Rev. 5:8)*. This was something independent, and was not accompanied by any animal sacrifice, and this remained in existence in the New Testament.

The raising of incense was not a ceremony only connected with animal sacrifice and conditioned by it, but was a spiritual activity, like the prayers of the saints, having an effectiveness all on its own.

[35]

CANDLES IN CHURCH

Question

Why do we light candles in church when there are electric lights?

Answer:

Candles are naturally for giving light. They were used in the past because they gave a soft, subdued light, and because this light inspired humility and awe to a greater extent than brighter, more glaring lights. This explains why we find churches which are lit by candles alone are more awe-inspiring.

They are used nowadays, although we have electric lights, in those special situations when we feel that the people need to concentrate specifically on the light.

They are used, for example, during the reading of the gospel, because we are seeking enlightenment from it, for the Bible says: *"Your word is a lamp to my feet and a light for my path. " (Ps. 119:105),* and also; *" The commandment of the LORD is pure, enlightening the eyes;" (Ps. 19:8).*

Candles are also placed before the icons of the saints, as an indication that a particular saint was a light to the world, and that like a candle he or she faded away in order to give light to others. And since the candle requires oil to burn, and oil symbolises the Holy Spirit, so the light of the candle suggests that the saint was not himself giving out light, but this was effected by the grace of the Holy Spirit within him.

We also light candles as a reminder of the presence of the angels, who are also lights and a fire that burns'. And there are two candlesticks which are placed on the altar as a reference to the two angels who are mentioned in the story of the Resurrection.

We light candles at particular moments during the divine Mass, especially during the prayers for sanctifying the sacraments, as a reminder of the presence of God Himself, who is the "True Light "who has come into the world to give light to all people. His advent meant the coming of light to the world.

When the deacons hold the candles in their hands, they are suggesting that the ministers of the church are bearing light to the world for divine guidance. They are to be seen as the torchbearers giving light just as the angels of God give light in heaven.

Candles in general suggest light, and suggest the life of devotion that God wants for mankind. The Bible likens goodness to light, and evil to darkness. The righteous are called the 'children of light', and the wicked the 'sons of darkness'. The Lord said: " *Walk while you have the light, lest darkness overtake you; he who walks in darkness does not know where he is going." (John 12:35)*

Light also indicates the transfiguration of the righteous as happened to Moses and Elijah on Mount Tabor and suggests the luminous bodies in which we will be raised in eternity.

The deacons carrying the candles behind the priest, or around him, remind us of the five wise maidens who carried their lamps with enough oil, as a reminder that we should always be prepared.

I wish that I could give you a whole book about the function of candles and lamps in church, as a subject on its own, and not just an answer to one question.

[36]

AT THE RIGHT HAND OF THE FATHER

Question

What proof is there that the Lord rose and is seated at the right hand of the Father, and where is this miracle mentioned?

Answer:

This miracle first comes in the gospel of St Mark.

It says at the end of it: *"After the Lord had spoken to them, He was received up into heaven, and sat down at the right hand of God." (Mark 16:19)*

It also comes in the Book of Acts, in more than one place. For example, after the Lord's last meeting with His disciples, when He said to them: *" you shall receive power when the Holy Spirit has come upon you; and you shall be witnesses to Me... "* and *" Now when He had spoken these things, while they watched, He was taken up, and a cloud received Him out of their sight "* And following this, two angels said to them: *" This same Jesus, who was taken up from you into heaven, will so* *come in like manner as you saw Him go into heaven."(Acts 1:8,9 & 11)*

It also comes in the vision of St. Stephen the deacon, when he was being stoned: *"Stephen, full of the Holy Spirit, looked up to heaven and saw the glory of God, and Jesus standing at the right hand of God. 'Look he said, 'I see heaven open and the Son of Man standing at the right hand of God." (Acts 7:55-56)*

There are many references to be found in the Book of Hebrews too. For example it says of Christ that: *"After He had provided purification for sins, He sat down at the right hand of the Majesty on high," (Heb. 1:3).*

And when St Paul was speaking about the Lord as the high priest, he said: *"The point of what we are saying is this: We do have such a high priest, who sat down at the right hand of the throne of Majesty in heaven" (Acts 8:1).*

And at the end of this epistle he said: " *looking unto Jesus, the author and finisher of our faith, who for the joy that was set before Him endured the cross, despising the shame, and has sat down at the right hand of the throne of God." (Heb. 12:2)*

The prophecy for this comes in the Psalms, where David was speaking in the Holy Spirit:

"The LORD said to my Lord, "Sit at My right hand, Till I make Your enemies Your footstool. " (Ps. 110:1)

The Lord's sitting at the right hand of God is something which I have dealt with elsewhere, in the first volume of this series.

[37]

ATONING FOR SINS

Question

If someone has sinned, should he atone for it by doing a good deed or by almsgiving?

Answer:

The Bible says: *"the wages of sin is death "* *(Rom. 6:23).* There is no escape from this death sentence, except through Christ's death on our behalf; for He is the only atonement for our sins. *(Rom. 3:24-5; 1 John 2:2, 4:10)*

Only a person who believes in this blood and this atonement is worthy to receive it *(John 3:16)*, providing he is repentant, and has received the grace of baptism *(Acts 2:38; Luke 13:3,5)*.

A person is not saved by his acts alone (without faith), whatever good deeds he might have done. The Bible says about the redemption given by Christ, *"Salvation is found in no-one else"* *(Acts:4.12)*.

As far as the action of mercy or almsgiving is concerned, it is that which moves the heart of God to pity, for the Lord Christ said: " *Blessed are the merciful, For they shall obtain mercy* " *(Matt. 5:7)* But the action of mercy without repentance and without faith, cannot save anyone. On account of mercy, however, God's grace can kindle a person's heart and call him to repentance, and if he repents he will be worthy of the blood of Christ and his sins will be forgiven.

[38]

WHEN SHOULD THE HOLY CHRISM (MYRON) BE MADE?

Question

The making of the Chrism, the Holy Myron used in baptism and consecration, was sometimes carried out in the sixth week of the Lent and sometimes in the Pascha (passion week). Which of them is more suitable?

Answer:

In actual fact, it is better not to make the Holy Myron during the Pascha days.

This is because the readings for preparing the unction are different from those for Holy Week, and their times are different too. Also the days of Passion Week are totally taken up with remembering the sufferings of Christ. So how can we properly divert our attention during this time to making the Holy Myron? These are also days of sorrow, while the making of the Myron requires more of a festival spirit, for which the piety of fasting, rather than the sadness of the Passion, is more appropriate. The original method dating from the time of St Athanasius was not to make it during the Holy Pascha.

[39]

THE MAKING OF THE HOLY MYRON IN THE MONASTERY OR IN THE PATRIARCHATE

Question

For a long time the making of the Holy Myron used to be carried out in one of the monasteries, and then it was transferred to the Patriarchate, where it remained for some time. Why was this? And why did it then go back to being made in the monasteries?

Answer:

A monastery is a very appropriate place for making the Holy Myron, firstly because it is a Holy place, and secondly, because it is far away from the noise and bustle of the city. So why did we take it to the Patriarchate in Cairo at all?

Well, that happened not because of a particular theological or ecclesiastical reason, but rather because of the problem of transport.

In the past, people had to reach the monasteries by camel, because there weren't any asphalt roads, as there are nowadays, on which their carts or vehicles could pass easily along the way and reach the monastery as easily and quickly as we can today.

The way across the desert sand by camel was hard, and took a long time. Just imagine what it must have been like for the rider on his camel, with the precious Holy Oil and the pre-baptismal or Ghalilaun shaking about in large glass containers with every step of the camel, and in constant danger of getting broken, and being spilt all over the place - and all this on a journey that lasted a long time!

It actually happened on one occasion that a huge container of oil was broken, but fortunately it was only one of Ghalilaun [*] and not the holy chrism. The Pope at that time was very upset by this and decided to make the Holy Oil in Cairo, and that is where it continued to be made from the time of the 89th Pope until recently.

Now circumstances have changed however, and the original difficulties of transportation which called for that change in the first place no longer exist, and there isn't the danger of large glass containers being broken, or their contents being spilt, because in fact plastic containers are now used to bottle the Holy Oil.

Therefore the making of the Holy Oil returned to the monasteries as before.

• for an explanation of this term see the following section

[40]

WHAT IS THE 'GHALILAUN'?

Question

We have heard that on Thursday 16 of April 1971, two kinds of Holy oil were consecrated one being the Myron and the other was Ghalilaun. What is the Ghalilaun? What is it used for? How is it made, and what does it mean to consecrate it?

Answer:

The word Ghalilaun which we use for this second kind of oil, comes from two Greek words joined together which mean 'oil of joy' or 'oil of happiness' or 'oil of rejoicing'.

This is the oil with which the person is anointed before his baptism, in the ritual of repudiating Satan, and its function is to ward off any bad spirits that might want to lead astray the one being anointed, or which might try to obstruct his faith, or plant blasphemous thoughts in his mind when he is an adult.

When the priest anoints the one being baptised with this type of oil, he says: 'I anoint you with the oil of joy... which was planted in the sweet olive tree before your baptism'.

In the past, the Church used to anoint those who were coming new to the faith, with this oil, to prepare them for seeking enlightenment and the sacrament of baptism. This is why it used to be called the oil of anointing and preparation.

The composition of the Ghalilaun is made up of three elements:

a) pure olive oil.

b) a number of drops from the sacred olive oil and our present stock contains the products of 23 batches of the holy chrism.

c) the ferment from the old Ghalilaun, which is formed in the bowl of the Ghalilaun by the boiling of the drops of chrism with the olive oil.

The special prayer which is said over the Ghalilaun to consecrate it is recited after a prayer for the chrism, and both His Holiness and the bishops take part in this. Then the Pope makes the sign of the cross over the Ghalilaun just as he has previously done over the holy chrism.

In the past, this oil - the oil of joy - was used to anoint kings and priests. It was formerly used to anoint, according to what the Lord commanded Moses, was composed of some of the constituents of the chrism, as it says in Exodus 30, though of course the chrism, now, is different, because spices, and grains from the embalming that was on the body of Christ, have since been added to it. These things were obviously not available in the Old Testament times, and it is in this respect that the chrism differs from the Ghalilaun.

[41]

WHERE SHOULD THE OFFERTORY BREAD BE PLACED?

Question

In some churches the plate containing the offertory bread is placed inside the sanctuary on a shelf or chair, and sometimes it is put on the altar after the Mass until the end of the prayer of blessing. Is this right?

Answer:

The **only** kind of bread that is permitted to enter the sanctuary is the Host which is the offering of bread which the priest prays over in the Mass to consecrate it in order to transubstantiate it for the believers to receive in the Communion.

If any other offering of bread should enter the sanctuary, that is a clear mistake. Or to put it more precisely, it is an even greater mistake if the plate of this unconsecrated bread is placed on the altar. The laws of the Church have defined what may be placed on the altar, since it is not an ordinary table !

The plate of the unconsecrated bread is to be placed outside the sanctuary, in a suitable place, since the sign of the cross is to be made over it outside the sanctuary. Then one is chosen to be consecrated, outside the sanctuary before the offertory is being presented.

[42]

WHEN SHOULD THE ORDINARY BREAD BE DISTRIBUTED?

Question

Some people take and eat the ordinary bread, which is to be given after the Mass, when they arrive at church, and eat it, or let their children actually eat it in the church during the service. Is this permitted? Or should we only take it on leaving the church after the end of the Mass?

Answer:

The correct thing to do is to take the bread as you depart from the church after the end of the Mass, and after you have heard the blessing and the dismissal.

Originally this custom arose because the people came to church fasting, and attended the Mass fasting, and so on their departure, the Church gave them the bread of blessing.

In olden times the churches used to hold an ' **agape**' or love meal, in which the people used to have their breakfast together, after they had left the church. There was a special or private room for this, and the more wealthy believers would take turns in providing such a meal, in the name of the Church. But this custom gradually died out, except for being held on a few special occasions. Finally, it was thought sufficient that the believer should be given a piece of bread on leaving the church, so that all could be said to have eaten from one meal - which was the bread.

But to distribute this bread before people enter the church doesn't make sense, and has no purpose from the pastoral point of view. It also gives some of the children the opportunity to eat it during the service, a thing which forbids them to take Communion!

[43]

THE DEACONS AND THE DISTRIBUTION OF THE EULOGIA

Question

Is it permitted for the deacons to break and distribute the portions of the bread of blessing (ie. the bread given to people after the Mass), to the people in the church, as happens in our Church ?

And is it permitted for this to take place while the priest is distributing the holy sacraments, in order to save time so that the people can leave more quickly?

Answer:

Only the priest is supposed to give out the portions of the bread of blessing (the Eulogia) to the congregation when they leave the church after the end of the Mass and following the recitation of the final blessing.

When the believers receive this Eulogia from the hand which was only minutes before, touching he body of Christ, it has a better effect on their hearts and they can feel conscious in taking a blessing from the hand of the Father, from the hand of the priest of God.

Also, when the priest distributes the Eulogia, it gives him a chance to see who has attended the service, and who has not, so that he can ask after them and perhaps pay them a visit. Sometimes it provides him with an opportunity to say a few words to various people, and for them to speak to him. These moments could be used for any useful purpose, offering the chance for him to congratulate, to give his condolences, to encourage, to pray for someone, to arrange an appointment with someone to pray about something, or arrange a visit.

It is also an opportunity for the people to receive the blessing of the priest and to say hello to him before they leave the church.

The wholly consecrated deacon, however, is one of them, one of the clergy after all, but generally speaking, it is rare nowadays to find such deacons who are entitled to wear clerical dress, and who have devoted themselves completely to the ministry. Most of the deacons in the church are only less in rank :-aghnastus (reader) or Epideacon (assisting deacon).

But as far as distributing this Eulogia during the sharing of the holy sacraments is concerned, this is something definitely unsuitable, for it would mean that attention was being diverted from the divine mysteries to something else, when the only thing that should be going on at that time is a hymn of praise.

The expression you mentioned, to 'save time' is an unacceptable excuse because this is essentially a spiritual situation, which is important, and demands attention. Time, however, can be recouped in other ways. It isn't right for us to do wrong from the spiritual point of view on the flimsy pretext of 'saving time'!

This is like someone who leaves church during the service, and even during its holy moments, to 'save time'!!

[44]

THE DEACONS AND TAKING COMMUNION

Question

Is it right for a deacon, who is wearing his tunic to attend the Mass, but not take Communion - on the excuse that he has been serving outside the sanctuary?

Is it allowed for the church reciter, the one who leads the deacons in singing, to serve and not take Communion?

Answer:

If a deacon does not take Communion, he is not supposed to wear the tunic, because it is a special garment for serving at the altar. So the deacon is not allowed to serve at the altar and not take Communion.

From the point of view of taking Communion, there exists no difference in the Church's rituals between a deacon who serves outside the sanctuary or inside it. They are all deacons and are supposed to be prepared to receive Communion, otherwise they would be a bad example to the people.

The only reasons for not taking Communion are: not having fasted, not having repented, or not being spiritually prepared, all of which also prevent one from serving as a deacon. So anything that disqualifies one from taking Communion also disqualifies one from serving as a deacon.

The whole congregation is supposed to come to church in a state of fasting, and spiritual preparation, because as the Reciter says in the Psalm: *"Holiness adorns Your house, O LORD . "(Ps. 93:5)*

In the past, all those who attended the Holy Mass, the Mass of the Saints, had prepared themselves to partake so there is all the more reason now for the deacons to attend and to wear their tunics!

For a deacon to attend just to sing the chants and then leave, this is something not permitted according to Church rules. If he doesn't wish to receive Communion, or is not prepared to do so, then the priest ought not to sign the cross over his tunic.

[45]

CAN A DEACON HOLD THE CHALICE DURING THE COMMUNION SERVICE?

Question

I received the following question from America: If there is a large number of people taking Communion, can a deacon help the priest by taking the chalice?

Answer:

If there is another priest in the church, then he is the one who should help with the Communion, and the deacon, in this situation, is not allowed to take the chalice since there is no pressing need for him to do so.

But if there is only one priest, then there exists a basic condition in which the deacon could perform this task and is permitted to do so, if in the circumstances the serving priest is unable to give Communion to all the people. This condition stipulates that:

The deacon should be wholly consecrated in order to be able to assist the priest, by virtue of his rank, and to be

completely devoted to the Church's ministry, and wear clerical dress.

He must be someone who doesn't have an ordinary job, or wear ordinary clothes outside the church, and he must be recognisable to the people as someone who has consecrated himself to the religious ministry. According to Church rules any bishop, priest or wholly consecrated deacon who involves himself in an outside job (that is, works outside the Church) should be cut off.

If the wholly consecrated deacon takes the chalice in a situation where there isn't another participating priest then he will not be offending the people at all.

It is not permitted, however, for deacons of any lesser rank to do so. This is because serving at the altar and receiving the holy sacraments, is not something everyone can do, but is only for those who have devoted themselves to the ministry, and each one should only undertake the duties appropriate to his rank.

[46]

A FUNERAL PROCESSION FOR A DEACON WHO HAS DEPARTED

Question

Is it right that a deacon who has departed is taken round the church in a procession, after his body has been prayed over, because when he was confirmed as a deacon, he had the bishop's hand laid upon him?

Answer:

It is well known that the priests are taken in procession (after they depart), around the altar which they have served, and to which they have dedicated their lives. But as far as a deacon is concerned, if he is a wholly consecrated deacon who has dedicated himself to the ministry, who has no other job apart from being a full deacon and who has been blessed by the bishop laying his hand upon him and who is entitled to wear clerical dress, then it is quite all right for his body to be taken in procession around the church, in view of the fact that he has devoted himself to its ministry.

But the lower ranks of deacon, from Chanter to Sub-deacon who have not received the hand of ordination upon them are not entitled to this procession, because they have not devoted themselves entirely to serving the altar.

[47]

PREACHING DURING COMMUNION

Question

Is it permitted for a sermon to be delivered during the distribution of Communion, when the believers are actually receiving the holy mysteries?

Answer:

No. It is something that is not allowed, because it would mean a lack of respect for these sacred moments and would cause a distraction from the sacraments.

While Communion is taking place, the only other appropriate activity to be going on is the singing of chants or hymns of praise. So the Church should apply itself, at that point, to praising God for the blessings which He has poured out on us so lavishly, in permitting us to partake of His holy body and blood.

If we were to be distracted from the word of God by the words of other people, then this would be neither permissible nor appropriate, because we would be neglecting the great sacrament present on the altar, and would be giving our thoughts and feelings to the subject of the sermon.

Let us not forget that people usually listen to the sermon when they are sitting down, whereas during Communion it is not suitable for people to be seated.

[48]

THE SUNDAY PRECEDING THE LENT AND GETTING MARRIED

Question

Is it possible to get married on the Sunday preceding.lent?

Answer:

The Patriarchate issued an instruction some years ago to all its churches to forbid marriages on the Sunday before Lent and the reason for this is that it would be likely to cause a breaking of the fast.

One could hardly expect the bridal couple to fast, either on the morning of their marriage, from the point of view of taking no food, or from the abstention from marital relations for 55 days straight after the marriage (this being the period of the Great Fast).

The Bible says: " *Can the friends of the bridegroom mourn as long as the bridegroom is with them? (Matt. 9:15)*

If we were to allow couples to get married on the Sunday before Lent, we would be implicitly permitting them to break the fast, which would not be right.

This same situation would apply to any period of fasting, which is why it is necessary for marriage to be prohibited at such times.

[49]

WHY WOMEN ARE NOT PERMITTED TO ENTER THE SANCTUARY

Question

Why aren't women permitted to enter the sanctuary? What difference is there between men and women in this respect?

Answer:

Basically, the only people allowed to enter the sanctuary are those who serve at the altar, and by them we mean the men of the priesthood and the deacons and no-one else.

Those who are not priests or deacons are not permitted to go into the area around the altar and it makes no difference whether they are men or women.

In some ancient churches, we have seen that they have an aperture in the veil of the sanctuary through which the believers receive the holy mysteries while they stand well outside the sanctuary area.

The reason that the sanctuary is raised up from floor level by three steps is because it is a symbol of the three degrees of priesthood by which those who minister at the altar ascend to the sanctuary.

Since women in the Coptic Church are not part of the clergy, they are not allowed to enter the sanctuary.

Thus there is no difference between men and women. One and the same rule applies to them both about their not being allowed to enter the sanctuary.

[50]

ABOUT WOMEN DURING MENSTRUATION TIME

Question

Is it allowed for a woman while menstruating to receive Communion, and if not, why not? Because after all, this is something natural which she can't help.

And if she just sits down at home, is she allowed to worship privately, to pray and read the Bible etc.?

Answer:

At home she can worship God however she likes at this time of the month, but if she takes Communion in church, or outside it, this is absolutely not allowed.

A person is not permitted to receive Communion if blood is flowing from his body, and this applies to both sexes, and it also applies to any secretion of a sexual nature: this is clear from the Bible.

There are many Biblical texts and many Church regulations which confirm this point and have made it clear for people to understand.

But someone might plead that it isn't fair on women, since nothing comparable applies to men. For when men have wet dreams or if any discharge comes from their bodies, they can still enter Church and no-one is likely to prevent them, and no rules can be enforced against them. So why should this happen to women?

Perhaps someone might ask that there are some men who aren't deacons but who nevertheless enter the sanctuary and take Communion. How is that so?

In actual fact, this was only ever permitted to the king who had been crowned in the Orthodox manner, and had been anointed with the holy oil in view of the fact that he was the Lord's anointed.

As for other people entering, perhaps they have another reason for doing so which could be one of the following:

Many of the men who do this have actually been admitted to one of the lower degrees of deacon, but might not be wearing their proper deacon's dress at the time that they enter the sanctuary, as they should, and this is a mistake which the Church is trying to remedy, by forbidding all deacons from entering the sanctuary, even those decreed to be at one of the lower levels, but who don't happen to be serving or wearing their tunics on that day.

But there is also another mistake which I have observed which has been necessitated really by a professional situation which is that some men, such as builders, engineers or decorators might need to enter the sanctuary during the course of their work, but this obviously wouldn't be during a service. In a similar way, it might be necessary at times for painters, television or radio men to enter the sanctuary.

The answer is that the most the man is permitted to do is to enter the church after having cleansed himself bodily, but he is not allowed to receive Communion.

There is a basic difference though between the kind of discharge coming from the man and the woman, which is that: the man's is incidental and temporary, whereas the woman's continues for several days. The following point, however, would make them both equal and that is if the man's discharge were continuous, he would also be forbidden to take the communion in exactly the same way.

But there remains the point that it is not the woman's fault, that it is something natural which she can't help.

No, it's nobody's fault: there is nothing wrong in it, and no-one is being blamed but God just wants to always remind us of the first sin of mankind.

If we are mindful of that first sin, we are more likely to value the ransom paid out for us.

The wages of sin is death, and even though Christ died for us, He still left us with a mark to remember this by, which is for men, that *"By the sweat of your brow you will eat your food" and for women, that "with pain you will give birth to children." (Gen. 3:19,18)*

In the case of pregnancy, the woman's menstruation stops, and she is reminded of Eve's original sin by the pains of pregnancy, birth and delivery, and outside the period of pregnancy she recalls her sin at the time of menstruation and this makes her realise how much her sins forbid her from receiving holy blessings, not only those which are associated with Communion and the Church.

Men, on the other hand, are reminded of their first sin because they are supposed to labour throughout their lives on account of earning their daily bread. The remembrance of this is the aim, though the means might vary enormously.

It would be better for us to try and derive spiritual benefit from thinking more deeply about the meaning of these things rather than complaining about them.

[51]

WHY WE BEATIFY THE VIRGIN MARY

Question

Why do we beatify our Lady, St. Mary? Is it because of her motherhood virginity or faith?

I heard one of the Plymouth Brethren say that we should not beatify the Virgin Mary, either as a mother or as a virgin, since physical motherhood was not the kind of motherhood that the Lord honoured! And that person also said that God didn't attach particular importance from the spiritual point of view, to natural family relationships or physical kinship, and that the only reason for us to beatify St. Mary would be for her faith. What is the Orthodox view on these matters?

Answer:

We beatify St. Mary for all these things: for being the mother of our Lord, for her virginity and faith, and for her holy life. We beatify her for all these things together, but especially because she was the mother of God. For she was singled out from among all the women in the world for this purpose.

We can say to her the words of the proverb: *"Many daughters have done well, But you excel them all. " (Prov. 31:29)*

In fact St. Elizabeth said to Virgin Mary: *"Blessed is she who believed, for there will be a fulfillment of those things which were told her from the Lord."(Luke 1:45)* And what Mary believed would be accomplished was that she would become the Mother of God. Elizabeth did not restrict Mary's beatification just to her having this faith, but had previously said: *" But why is this granted to me, that the mother of my Lord should come to me?" (Luke 1:43).* And in praising St. Mary she added: *"Blessed are you among women, and blessed is the child you will bear!" (Luke 1:43)*

All these things focus on St Mary being the Mother of God, and we cannot just take one phrase of Elizabeth's glorification of St Mary and leave out all the other references which go to provide a complete picture.

I would like to say that St Mary being a virgin and the Mother of God were two qualities which she possessed which were connected with the subject of salvation itself.

Salvation could not have come about without the incarnation and the incarnation meant that the Lord was born of a woman, from a human being, with the same nature that we possess, and by this it became possible for Him to act on our behalf. This is why the Lord Jesus Christ insisted on calling Himself the 'Son of Man', because it was in this capacity that He redeemed mankind. The only way that He could become a son of Man was through being born of St Mary.

Thus St Mary's special title of 'Mother of God' is a title that is connected with the redemption or the salvation, because this would not have come about if it hadn't been for the incarnation.

Does St Mary's virginity also have a connection with the subject of salvation?

Yes, of course, because Christ could not have been born as a result of normal human seed of man and woman, for this would have made Him an ordinary human being!

He had to be born of a virgin by some unusual method, through the Holy Spirit. He already had a Father, who was God, and thus He was not born in the state of original sin. And because He was holy, He was able to ransom sinners.

Why then should we not beatify the Virgin Mary for being a Virgin and the Mother of God when these two attributes were so necessary for our salvation?

In any case, would a person, whatever his Christian denomination, gain anything from not beatifying the Virgin Mary for being a virgin and the Mother of God? St. Paul praised virginity and said that it was a preferable state to marriage if the individual could manage it. *(See 1 Cor. 7)*

Therefore, when St. Mary said: *"From now on all generations will call me blessed"* **she did not mean that her faith would be the cause of her beatification, but that it was**

because, " *For He who is mighty has done great things for me, and holy is His name.* " *(Luke 1:48-49)*

Naturally this glorification was the ability to give birth, even though she was a virgin, to bear the Lord Himself. What glory could be greater than this?

Any woman can have faith. But it is not every woman who can bear a child whilst still a virgin and bear the child who was to be the Lord Himself!

So if the beatification of St Mary is confined to her faith alone, it would be to make her like other devout women, without being different from them at all, which is the familiar Protestant standpoint.

As far as God's not attaching particular spiritual importance to family relationships of physical kinship is concerned, that is not technically correct from what the Bible teaches.

Sufficient proof of this is that God put honouring one's parents as the top priority regarding the commandments pertaining to relationships between people. *(Deut. 5:16)*

St. Paul also stressed this commandment to honour your father and mother," *which is the first commandment with promise:*" *(Eph. 6:2)*

In the Old Testament, death was the penalty for cursing one's father or mother *(Matt. 15:4)*, and in the New Testament, it says: " *if anyone does not provide for his own, and especially for those of his household, he has denied the faith and is worse than an unbeliever* " *(1 Tim. 5:8)*. And the Lord Jesus Christ rebuked the Scribes and the Pharisees for not teaching the need to respect one's parents, on the pretext that anything that they might have given to their parents they were giving to God instead. *(Matt. 15:5)*

Something which perhaps gives a good indication of Christ's concern for His mother is that He singled her out when He was on the cross, with two out of the seven phrases that He said, and put her in the care of His beloved disciple. *(John 19:26-27)*

There are countless examples of the Lord's concern for family relationships.

To say that God attaches little spiritual importance to natural family bonds and ties of kinship would be to demolish the family and with it, the basis of society, which is something that would not agree with the teaching of the Bible, either in the Old Testament or the New. If someone does not respect his mother and father, he would be hardly likely to show respect for anyone else! They would be a disobedient and disrespectful son or daughter. Under the law of Moses the person would have been stoned and according to the New Testament he would not be regarded as a believer.

Finally, Christ honoured Virgin Mary as a mother and as a spiritual human being when He chose her for being the most holy woman of all, to be a Mother to Him ✧✧✧

[52]

CONCERNING HONOURING THE BODY OF THE VIRGIN MARY

Question

One of the Plymouth Brethren said that the body of the Virgin Mary was not different from that of any other believer, and that her earthly body must have been subjected to decay and decomposition. Also the writer denies that Mary's body ascended. What is your view?

Answer:

The Virgin's body was distinct from any human's body, and had its own special dignity, because it was the body in which the Lord of Glory spent nine months, and which the Holy Spirit sanctified with His coming upon it to place the Lord within. *(Luke 1:35)*

Is it likely that God would then leave that special body to decay and decompose, to be eaten by worms and rot without being honoured or respected, when He is the one who has honoured the bodies of so many of the saints?!

And would that body, which was the purest body that a human being ever had, not receive a special honour after death from the Lord?

Those who do not honour the Virgin Mary and who also do not honour the rest of the saints are ignorant of what the Lord said of His saints, that those who honoured them were also honouring Him.

The body of the Virgin will not only be honoured after the Resurrection, by being clothed in a glorious body, but has already been honoured by the Lord after her death. The Lord in a similar way, honoured the body of Moses before the Resurrection, when He let it appear on the Mount of Transfiguration. The question of the ascent of St. Mary's body is one that history records, and which history cannot deny. It is not just we who record it, but many other churches too.

Those who attack the Virgin gain nothing but actually lose a blessing.

[53]

IS THE VIRGIN THE "GATEWAY" TO LIFE?

Question

I read that one of the Plymouth Brethren had made an attack which was very insulting, upon the title given to the Virgin Mary in the Agpia (the prayer book of the Coptic Church), of the 'gateway to life' or the 'gateway to heaven'. He based his argument on the fact that the Lord Christ is the only gate that leads to life,, according to what the Lord Christ said of Himself: *"the gate for the sheep."* *(John 10:9-10)*. How should one reply to this?

Answer:

Calling the Lord Christ a 'gate' has one meaning, and calling St. Mary a 'gate' or 'gateway', has a different one.

The Lord Christ gave us many of His own titles which have various meanings. For example He said: "you are the light of the world " yet He also said of Himself: "I am the light of the world " But He, of course, is the truest light of all, whilst the light that we have, is derived from His. In the same way, the

Virgin being a 'gate' or 'gateway' does not prevent Christ's being the 'gate' for the sheep.

The name 'gate' or 'gateway' has also been applied to the Church, to prayer, to faith, to preaching the gospel and to all spiritual means of reaching God.

None of this, however, has detracted anything from Christ or His saving work. These titles, as we will see, are mentioned in the Bible, so they accord with the biblical truth which they defend.

The first church in the world to be consecrated was called the 'gate of heaven'.

Jacob, the Patriarch, said of the place in which he saw a ladder leading up to heaven from the earth: *"How awesome is this place! This is none other than the house of God; this is the gate of heaven. "* (Gen. 28:17), and he called that place 'Bethel' which means 'house of God'.

Does the Church being the 'gate of heaven' prevent Christ from also being a gate, ie. a way in, or a way leading to heaven?

The Church is a gate leading to Christ, and Christ is a gate leading to salvation and to the Father. The name is the same but the meaning is different.

The Virgin Mary, however, can also be regarded as a gateway, because she connected Christ to us through the body, and she was referred to as a 'gate' in the Book of

Ezekiel, where it says that the gate of the east has been shut, and "*It is to remain shut because the Lord, the God of Israel, has entered through it.* " *(Ez. 44:3)*

Prayer, too, has been called a gateway to heaven, because heaven is opened by prayer.

The Virgin Mary is not merely a gateway to heaven, but is in fact a kind of heaven herself.

Heaven is, after all, the dwelling place of God, and the Virgin became a dwelling place for God when He grew within her womb for nine months. Thus she became a 'heaven' for Him.

This is why the Church calls her the 'second heaven'. Because the Church has become a house of God, it too can be likened to heaven. Therefore we say in one of our prayers: When we stand in your holy temple (ie. in church), we consider ourselves to be standing in heaven.

The Bible mentions that there are gates which lead to heaven. For example it says: " *Blessed are those who do His commandments, that they may have the right to the tree of life, and may enter through the gates into the city.*" *(Rev. 22:14)* But does the existence of these gates prevent Christ from being a gate too?

All spiritual means can be gateways, provided they connect us to Christ, who is the only gate which leads to salvation through His blood.

The Lord spoke of this matter when He said: *"Because narrow is the gate and difficult is the way which leads to life, and there are few who find it." (Matt. 7:14)*

Do the Lord's words about the narrow gate prevent Him from being a gate too?

" The letter kills but the Spirit gives life. " (1 Cor. 3:6) We must always remember to understand the words of the Lord, and prayers of the Church, for their spiritual and not simply their literal meaning, as *"expressing spiritual truths in spiritual words. " (2 Cor. 2:13)*

Prayer and faith are both gates that can lead to God.

Saul and Barnabas came to Antioch and called together the Church: *" Now when they had come and gathered the church together, they reported all that God had done with them, and that He had opened the door of faith to the Gentiles. " (Acts 14:27)* It was this 'door of faith' that was their means to salvation, because it brought them into contact with Christ.

Preaching can also be a gateway leading to salvation, because it leads to faith, and faith then leads to Christ.

It was probably this gate which the Lord had in mind when He said to the angel of the church of Philadelphia *"I know your works. See, I have set before you an open door, and no one can shut it; " (Rev. 3:8)*

So if prayer, faith, preaching the gospel, the Church and the Virgin Mary can all be gateways leading to Christ, then *"Blessed are those who... may go through the gates into the city" which is of course, heaven. (Rev. 22:14)*

The Virgin Mary was the gate through which Christ came in order to save the world. Who was Christ?

1. Christ was the Messiah, and He was Life, according to what He said of Himself: *"I am the Resurrection and the life." (John 11:25),* and *"I am the way, the truth and the life." (John 14:6).*

So we can see how St. Mary can be called a 'gateway to life", by virtue of her being the very gate through which the Messiah - who is life, came into the world.

2. Christ is also the Redeemer and 'our salvation'. We sing in the psalm: *"The Lord is my strength and my song; And He has become my salvation." (Ps. 118:14)* So if Christ was and is a 'salvation' to the world, then there is nothing strange in our calling the gateway through which He came, that is the Virgin Mary the 'gate of salvation'!

[54]

YOU ARE THE TRUE VINE

Question

The Lord Christ said, "*I am the true vine*" *(John 15:1)*, so how can we say to the Virgin Mary in the prayers of the Agpia, 'You are the true vine that carries the fruit of life'? Are we to apply the same title to Mary as we do to Christ?

Answer:

When the Lord Jesus Christ says, "I am the true vine", it has a different meaning from when we say that St Mary is a 'true vine'. The word 'vine' can also be applied to the Church, to the people and to the individual human soul, as the Bible itself makes clear.

The Bible gives the title of 'vine' to the Church and it says in the psalm: " *Return, we beseech You, O God of hosts; Look down from heaven and see, And visit this vine* " *(Ps. 80:14)*, and we use these words in the Church's hymns.

The Lord Himself gave this title to the Church when He said: "*In that day - 'Sing about a fruitful vineyard: I, the Lord,* *watch over it; I water it continually.* ' " *(Is. 27:2)* and also: " *And now, O inhabitants of Jerusalem and men of Judah, Judge, please, between Me and My vineyard. What more could have been done to My vineyard That I have not done in it? Why then, when I expected it to bring forth good grapes, Did it bring forth wild grapes?" (Is. 5:3-4)*

So we see here that the Lord gave the name of 'vine' even to His people who had done wrong and borne bad fruit!

We also see Him referring to Israel as: " *'Your mother was like a vine in your bloodline, Planted by the waters, Fruitful and full of branches Because of many waters. But she was plucked up in fury, She was cast down to the ground, And the east wind dried her fruit. Her strong branches were broken and withered; The fire consumed them." (Ezek. 19:10,12)*

And in the Book of Joel He makes another reference to Israel when He says: "*He has laid waste My vines and ruined My fig-trees. " (Joel 1:7)*

When the Lord compared His people or the Church to a vine He said: " *There was a certain landowner who planted a vineyard and set a hedge around it, dug a winepress in it and built a tower. And he leased it to vinedressers and went into a far country. " (Matt. 21:33)*

Here the Lord likened the Church to a vine, and the vinedressers to the Father, saying: "*I am the true vine, and My Father is the vinedresser. " (John 15:1)* But of course when the word vine is used of Christ it has a different meaning from when it is used to refer to the Church.

The Bible even uses the word vine to refer to women, when it says: "*Your wife shall be like a fruitful vine In the very heart of your house, Your children like olive plants All around your table.* " *(Ps. 128:3)*

So if the word 'vine' can be given to a woman or a wife, to the people of God, even when they have gone astray, and can be given to the Church as a whole, what is wrong with using it for the Virgin Mary, whom we also call the 'second heaven'?

We see many cases where God's titles are actually used for man and for nature.

The Lord said: "*I am the light of the world*" *(John 8:12)*, and said to His disciples: "You are the light of the world " thus using the same name, though in both cases it means different things, quite apart from the word 'light' when used to refer to real, physical. "*God said, 'Let there be light,' and there was light. God saw that the light was good, and He separated the light from the darkness.* " *(Gen. 1:3)*

And the word of God is also called a 'light': "*Your word is a lamp to my feet and a light to my path.* " *(Ps. 119:105)*

[55]

THE VIRGIN MARY AS 'WALL'

Question

Is it right for us to refer to the Virgin Mary as 'the wall of our salvation'?

One of the Plymouth Brethren has cast doubt about this designation, which comes from the words of the prophet Isaiah: *"but you will call your walls Salvation "* (Is. 60:18). Did St Mary rise to the rank of being a 'salvation'?

Answer:

The Bible does not just consist of one verse but is a whole book full of them.

Anyone who uses one verse to the exclusion of. the others which relate to it, is not giving a true picture of what the Bible is saying, nor is he giving the full meaning of Divine Inspiration.

The word "wall" in the Bible is used to mean protection.

Thus one of Nabal the Carmelite's servants said to Abigail: " *They were a wall to us both by night and day, all the time we were with them keeping the sheep.* " *(1 Sam. 25:16)*, meaning that they had protected and defended them.

It was in this sense that "the walls of Jerusalem" were looked to for protection from one's enemies, and the phrase 'a city without walls' came to mean one that was open to its enemies, without any protection or defence.

But let us see whether God is the only one who has been specially referred to as being a 'wall', or whether this word has also been applied to human beings.

This title has in fact been used for certain people, perhaps the best example we have is that of Jeremiah, of whom the word of God said: " *And I will make you to this people a fortified bronze wall, ...* " *(Jer. 15:20)*

If God Himself appointed this prophet to be a protector for the people, to the extent that He called him a "wall" for them, and a strong wall at that, then it is not contrary to faith for the Virgin to be regarded as a wall, because she was in every way more important than Jeremiah.

The Lord confirmed this purpose of His to Jeremiah himself when He said to Him: " *I have made you this day A fortified city and an iron pillar, And bronze walls against the whole land; Against the kings of Judah, Against its princes, Against its priests, And against the people of the land.* " *(Jer. 1:18)*

What an amazing thing it was, that Jeremiah be a wall to all the land!
The bride in the Song of Songs is also referred to as a 'wall':

" I am a wall, And my breasts like towers; then I became in his eyes as one who found peace." (Song 8:10) If we consider the bride here to stand for the Church, then the Church can be regarded as a wall for believers, to protect them from falling.

We have obtained salvation through the blood of Christ, and what we have obtained and now have, requires prayers to protect it and to be a wall surrounding it, so that we do not fall, through lack of faith.

No prayers are more powerful than those of the Virgin Mary, the Mother of God, the 'wall of our salvation'.

[56]

WAS THE VIRGIN MARY EVER A BRIDE?

Question

I read a vehement criticism from one of the Plymouth Brethren concerning reference to the Virgin Mary as a 'bride', in which it argued that the Church, and not the Virgin, was the 'bride'. Please would you clarify this for us.

Answer:

It is true that the Church has been called the bride of Christ, as John the Baptist put it, but all human souls have also been called the 'brides' of the Lord.

From this whole number of brides the greatest bride was made, and in the same situation and in the same sense, the Church has been called the 'Virgin'. For example, see what St Paul says: " *For I am jealous for you with godly jealousy. For I have betrothed you to one husband, that I may present you as a chaste virgin to Christ.* " *(2 Cor. 11:2)*. Here the Church is the Virgin, the bride of Christ, and at the same time the Bible speaks of every living soul as a maiden in love, saying: "*Therefore the virgins love you*" *(Song 1:3)*

Thus the fact that the Church is the bride of Christ does not preclude each living soul from being a Virgin bride to Christ, according to the Bible.

It was Christ Himself who gave us this teaching, when He said that the kingdom of heaven was like the five wise virgins who went out ready and prepared to meet the bridegroom, and so were able to enter into the wedding feast with him.

Those wise virgins are a symbol for each bride of Christ.

The Bible does not say that only one chaste virgin was betrothed to Christ, who waited for Him and entered into the wedding feast to delight herself in Him as her husband, but it uses the plural 'virgins' to stand for all human souls individually.

What is said of the Church here can apply to every person.

Every girl who dedicates herself to the Lord can call herself a bride of Christ.

The same goes for every soul that loves Him, whether male or female, they are also Christ's brides, and will wait to enter with Him into the heavenly wedding feast. We cannot strike out any soul from loving the Lord, and say that there can only be one bride for Him which is the Church.

The Song of Songs gives us the best and clearest illustration of this truth.

We cannot prevent anyone from meditating on the words of this Song, nor say to them that it only symbolises the Church and not individuals.

In actual fact, the Song of Songs contains expressions which could not possibly be applied to the Church, but when used to refer to human beings, and when seen in the context of personal relationships, become entirely appropriate, such as the words of the bride: "*I slept but my heart is awake... my beloved had turned away and was gone... . I sought him, but I could not find him .* " *(Song 5:2,6)* It would be difficult to describe the Church as sleeping or refusing to open itself to the Lord, and the Lord turning His back on her and leaving her, and then her searching for Him and not finding Him, her calling for Him and His not answering. These words are really only appropriate in the context of personal human relationships, and in particular, for people who are in a lowered or weak spiritual state.

The word 'bride' is familiar to us from the Song of Songs.

"*How fair is your love, My sister, my spouse!.. Your lips, O my spouse, Drip as the honeycomb;... A garden enclosed Is my sister, my spouse, A spring shut up, A fountain sealed." (Song 4:10-12)*

We observe how in these verses the word 'bride' is used without any difference and to convey the same meaning.

The words of this Song could possibly refer in some places to the Church, but in most cases it simply refers to the love between human beings.

It is difficult for us to determine the exact meaning or context of these words of the Bible.

It isn't easy for us just to draw a narrow circle around them and say: " this particular passage only has one meaning," when if we were to meditate upon it, we might find in it endless possibilities.

As an example of this there are the seven letters to the seven churches in the Book of Revelation, which are sometimes taken to be letters to specific churches during the lifetime of St John, and at other times are regarded as letters to any church at any time, which might be passing through a similar experience, and yet they can also be taken more personally, as letters addressed to all individual believers.

The word of God is limitless, and David was right when he said: *" I have seen the consummation of all perfection, But Your commandment is exceedingly broad." (Ps. 119:96)*

If the word 'bride' can be applied to any human being then why shouldn't it be even more appropriate to the Virgin?

Is there anything wrong with that, which should make a person get zealously worked up to attack it? That writer you mention, wastes his time writing about it, and other people's time in having to refute it! And he also raises doubts in some people's minds, when there are subjects from the Bible that are far more essential, which need to be dealt with, either rejected or defended, and especially when the whole Bible is accused of being false or of distorting things!

Is this really so much of a problem that we need to ask wether these words refer to a human being or to the Church? Is not the human being in a sense, a Church also.

Doesn't the Bible say: " *Do you not know that you are the temple of God and that the Spirit of God dwells in you? If anyone defiles the temple of God, God will destroy him. For the temple of God is holy, which temple you are.. " (1 Cor. 3:16-17)*

So a human being can be a small church, and from the totality of these small churches the universal Church is made up. It is the bride of Christ, and all these brides together form the largest bride of all which is the Church, the body of Christ.

It is perfectly all right for us to address each and every pure soul, and not only the Virgin Mary, with the words, 'You have found favour, O bride'.

And what about St Mary highly favoured one!

[57]

IS THE VIRGIN MARY A 'SISTER' TO US?

Question

I read in a book by one of the Plymouth Brethren that the Virgin Mary is a 'sister' to us! What is your opinion on this phrase?

Answer:

The Brethren tend to use the word 'brother' to apply to everybody, even the apostles and prophets, and while we are all children of Adam and Eve, there are still differences between us. Some are children, some are fathers and mothers, and the Bible says: *"Honour your father and your mother". (Ex. 20..12)* So we don't call our parents our brothers or sisters, even though they, like us, are still children of Adam and Eve.

Just as physical sonship exists, so does spiritual.

See how St John the Beloved said: " *My little children, these things I write to you, so that you may not sin." (1 John 2:1)* Since we look to St John as a spiritual father to us, we can hardly call him our 'brother'.

If St John as a father and apostle could say to us 'dear children', what about the Virgin Mary then?

The Lord called her a mother to His disciple John, who was himself a father to us, and so Mary has become through this situation a mother to us all.

Would it then be courteous for anyone to call her a 'sister'?

If no-one could call their own real mother by the title of 'sister' because the Bible instructs them to respect his mother then how much more should they respect the Virgin and call her mother, since she is the mother of all?

St Mary is not only a mother to us, but is also a mother to the Lord Himself.

St Elizabeth, who was an old woman, old enough to be St. Mary's mother, humbled herself before St. Mary and said to her: *"But why is this granted to me, that the mother of my Lord should come to me?" (Luke 1:43)* And it happened, when St Elizabeth heard the greeting of St Mary, that the babe leaped in her womb; and Elizabeth was filled with the Holy Spirit. *(Luke 1:41)*

If St Mary was a mother to the Lord, and He submitted obediently to her, as the Bible says *(Luke 2:51)*, how can we call her a 'sister'? After all there is something known as priority

The Lord Christ called us His brothers, and said that He was the first born among many brothers, and He addressed the two Marys after the Resurrection, saying: " *Do not be afraid. Go and tell My brethren to go to Galilee, and there they will see Me* " *(Matt. 28:10),* just as He also said: " *For whoever does the will of My Father in heaven is My brother and sister and mother.* " *(Matt. 12:50)*

So according to this, are we entitled to call Christ our 'brother', or treat Him like a brother, or address Him like a brother?

When speaking about St Mary, therefore, we must do so with the proper respect due to her. After all the angel Gabriel spoke to her with respect when he said: " *Rejoice, highly favored one, the Lord is with you; blessed are you among women!* " *(Luke 1:28)* And St Elizabeth addressed her with even more reverence and humility when she said: "why am I so favoured, that the mother of my Lord should come to me?"

So, when talking about St Mary we should do the same. Put before you the words of the Bible:

" **Render therefore to all their due: taxes to whom taxes are due, customs to whom customs, fear to whom fear, honor to whom honor.** " *(Rom. 13:7)*

That particular 'Brother' who regarded the Virgin Mary as a sister of his - when she was and is in fact the mother of Christ - is, if you think about it, actually putting himself in the position of Christ's uncle! ✥✥✥

[58]

DID THE VIRGIN MARY KNOW?

Question

Did the Virgin Mary know that Christ was the Son of God? And if so, did she realise that before the birth after it or because of Christ's miracles?

Answer:

St. Mary believed in Christ's divinity, and that He was God's son, before His birth, right from the time of the Annunciation when the angel said to her: " *that Holy One who is to be born will be called the Son of God.. " (Luke 1:35)*.

And St Elizabeth confirmed this fact when Virgin Mary visited her after becoming pregnant, and she said to Mary: ""*Blessed are you among women, and blessed is the fruit of your womb!" (Luke 1:43)* This shows that it was not only St Mary's belief, but Elizabeth's belief too. And this was evidence of Mary's faith.

In addition to all this, the miracles which Christ performed and the holy visions on the occasion of His birth, were things seen by St Mary besides all this.

I can confidently say that the Virgin Mary was the first person to believe in the divine nature of Christ.

Let us not forget that St. Mary had studied the Bible and knew the prophecy of Isaiah where it says: *"The virgin shall conceive and bear a Son, and shall call His name Immanuel." (Is. 7:14)* and also: *" For unto us a Child is born, Unto us a Son is given; And the government will be upon His shoulder. And His name will be called Wonderful, Counselor, Mighty God, Everlasting Father, Prince of Peace." (Is. 9:6)*

St. Mary understood that these holy verses applied to her and her son, and that all the wonderful things which were happening before her eyes confirmed this. It was these things which she was said to have treasured in her heart.

It was on account of this that Mary said: *"henceforth all generations will call me blessed. " (Luke 1:48)*

As for the second person who believed, that was St. Joseph the carpenter and that happened as a result of the angel's prophecy to him.

The third person was, of course Elizabeth and the fourth was John the Baptist, who suddenly leaped for joy in the womb of his mother because he was still within her at the time when Mary came to visit and when Jesus was a tiny seed inside her.✣✣✣

[59]

DID CHRIST HAVE ANY REAL BROTHERS?

Question

Who was James the brother of the Lord? Did the Lord Christ have any real brothers who were also born to Virgin Mary? If not, who were those brothers mentioned?

Answer:

James the brother of the Lord was James the son of Alphaeus and was at the same time Jesus' cousin according to the flesh, being the son of Jesus' maternal aunt who was Mary, the wife of Clopas. (Clopas was also named Alphaeus).

Children of one's maternal aunt were at that time regarded as one's brothers and sisters on the strength of this close tie of kinship according to the Jewish custom when one spoke of those born in the relationship.

For example, there is what the Bible says about the relationship of Jacob to his uncle Laban: *"When Jacob saw Rachel the daughter of Laban his mother's brother, and the sheep of*

Laban his mother's brother, that Jacob went near and rolled the stone from the well's mouth, and watered the flock of Laban his mother's brother. Then Jacob kissed Rachel, and lifted up his voice and wept. And Jacob told Rachel that he was her father's relative and that he was Rebekah's son. So she ran and told her father." (Gen. 29:10-12)

We see here that even though Laban was Jacob's uncle, Jacob was considered to be of Laban's 'own flesh and blood'.

We find that Laban also refers to Jacob as being one of his relatives when he invited him to look after his flocks: "*Because you are my relative, should you therefore serve me for nothing? Tell me, what should your wages be. (Gen. 29:15)*

The same thing happened regarding the relationship between Abraham and Lot.

Abraham was Lot's paternal uncle, and so the Bible said concerning the genealogy of the father of Abram and Haran (Lot's father) "*Terah took his son Abram and his grandson Lot the son of Haran" (Gen.11:31)*. Nevertheless, when Lot left Sodom during the war against Kedorlaomer, the Bible says: " *They also took Lot, Abram's brother's son who dwelt in Sodom, and his goods, and departed.... Now when Abram heard that his brother was taken captive, he armed his three hundred and eighteen trained servants who were born in his own house, and went in pursuit as far as Dan." (Gen 14:12-14)*

So it was on account of these ancient customs that the sons of Christ's maternal aunt, Mary the wife of Clopas, were called Jesus' brothers and sons of Mary.

It was about this Mary, the wife of Clopas, that the Bible said: " *Now there stood by the cross of Jesus His mother, and His mother's sister, Mary the wife of Clopas, and Mary Magdalene." (John 19:25).* And this was the Mary mentioned by Mark when he said: " *There were also women looking on from afar, among whom were Mary Magdalene, Mary the mother of James the Less and of Joses, and Salome,. " (Mark 15:40)*

This James, Joses and Salome were all children of Mary the wife of Clopas, and it was they who were mentioned in what the Jews were saying about Christ: " *Is this not the carpenter's son? Is not His mother called Mary? And His brothers James, Joses, Simon, and Judas?" (Matt. 13:55; Mark 6:3)*

As for the Virgin Mary, she gave birth only to the Lord Christ, and then lived as a virgin for the rest of her life, and so the 'brothers' of Christ mentioned above were not her children, but those of her sister.

James the younger (the son of Alphaeus), was called the ' younger' to distinguish him from James the elder (the son of Zebedee) the brother of John the Beloved.

[60]

THE RELATIONSHIP BETWEEN MARY AND ELIZABETH

Question

Since our Lady Mary was from the house of David, from the tribe of Judah, why did the angel Gabriel say to her: " *Elizabeth your relative has also conceived a son* " *(Luke 1:36)*, when Elizabeth, the wife of Zechariah the priest, was from the tribe of Levi, and descended from the daughter of Aaron? *(Luke 1:5)*.

Answer:

Some people take the word 'relative' in a wide sense in the same way that Paul used the word 'brothers' when speaking about the Jews as a whole: "*... my brothers, those of my own race, the people of Israel.* " *(Rom. 9:3-4)*

St. Severus, the Patriarch of Antioch, however, had a different point of view.

He said that when the angel who appeared to Joseph in a dream called him, "*Joseph son of David.* " *(Matt. 1:20)*, it was to remind him of God's previous promise, that the Messiah would come from the descendants of David. It was with a similar intent that the words *"Elizabeth your relative"*, which were addressed to Mary, were used to remind us of the link between Elizabeth and the distant past.

In actual fact it was written in the Book of Exodus, before the commandment which prohibited the taking of a wife from another tribe had been given, that Aaron, the first high priest, according to the Law, had *"married Elisheba (whose name meant Elizabeth) daughter of Amminadab and sister of Nahshon. "* *(Ex. 6:23)* and Nahshon was, *"the leader of the children of Judah. " (1 Chr. 2:10; Matt. 1:4)*

Look at the unfolding of the wise design of God's holy plan, and see how it was arranged that the wife of Zechariah was called Elizabeth, the mother of John the Baptist, and was a relative of Mary, the Mother of God. We can trace it all back to Elisheba (or Elizabeth), whom Aaron married, and through whom came the union of the two tribes and by whom this Elizabeth became a close relative of the Virgin Mary.

CONTENTS

Introduction
1. The Spirits and Their Work
2. Can the Spirits Recognise Each Other?
3. No-one Has Ever Seen God
4. How Can Spirits See Spirits?
5. The Crown of Righteousness
6. Who Are the Seraphim?
7. Justified Freely By His Grace
8. Concerning the Jewish Religion
9. Praying for the Deceased
10. Is there an Eternity for the Wicked and for Satan?
11. Did God Need Christ in Order to Create and to Save Mankind?
12. The Relationship of the Apostles with the Holy Spirit
13. How Can I Tell Which leaflets are Orthodox and Which are Not?
14. Concerning the Divinity of Christ
15. Is there Life on the Other Planets?
16. Replying to a Question with a Verse
17. Questions About the Holy Spirit
18. Was the Holy Spirit the Angel Gabriel?
19. Why are there Seven Mysteries (Sacraments)?
20. Are the Sacraments Necessary for All People?
21. Is the Sacrament Still the Same When a Shortened Service is Used?
22. The Point of Transubstantiation in the Sacrament of the Eucharist
23. About the Prayer of the Anointing of the Sick being Said in Homes

24. The Number of Heavens
25. Can Satan Enter a Church?
26. Fasting and Eating Fish
27. The Ascent into Heaven and the Earth's Gravity
28. Why the Cross?
29. God's Justice and Mercy
30. About Being Re-Baptised
31. Is There a Third Place for Worshipping God?
32. Has Satan Been Released From his Prison, and is the Last Day Approaching?
33. Who Are the Seventh-day Adventists?
34. Was the Use of Incense Abolished in the New Testament?
35. Candles in Church
36. At the Right Hand of the Father
37. Atoning for Sins
38. When Should the Holy Chrism (Myron) be ' Made?
39. The Making of the Holy Myron in the Monasteries or in the Patriarchate
40. What is the 'Ghalilaun'?
41. Where Should the Offertory Bread be Placed?
42. When Should the Ordinary Bread be Distributed?
43. The Deacons and the Distribution of the Eulogia
44. The Deacons and Taking Communion
45. Can a Deacon Hold the Chalice During the Communion Service?
46. A Funeral Procession for a Deacon Who Has Departed
47. Preaching During the Communion
48. The Sunday Preceding the Lent and Getting Married
49. Why Women are not Permitted to Enter the Sanctuary
50. About Women During Menstruation Time

51. Why do we Beatify the Virgin Mary?
52. Concerning the Honouring of the Body of the Virgin Mary
53. Is the Virgin the 'Gateway' to Life?
54. You are the 'true Vine'
55. The Virgin Mary as a 'Wall'
56. Was the Virgin Mary Ever a Bride?
57. Is the Virgin Mary a 'Sister' to Us?
58. Did the Virgin Mary Know?
59. Did Christ Have Any Real Brothers?
60. The Relationship Between Mary and Elizabeth.